YOU WILL DIE
IN PRISON

YOU WILL DIE IN PRISON

Bernard Phelan

eriu

First published by Eriu
An imprint of Black & White Publishing Group
A Bonnier Books UK company

4th Floor, Victoria House,
Bloomsbury Square,
London, WC1B 4DA

Owned by Bonnier Books
Sveavägen 56, Stockholm, Sweden

𝕏 – @eriu_books
⬚ – @eriubooks

Hardback – 978-1-80418-905-4
Trade paperback – 978-1-80418-906-1
Ebook – 9781-80418-907-8

A CIP catalogue of this book is available from the British Library.

Typeset by IDSUK (Data Connection) Ltd
Printed and bound by Clays Ltd, Elcograf S.p.A.

1 3 5 7 9 10 8 6 4 2

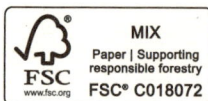

MIX
Paper | Supporting
responsible forestry
FSC
www.fsc.org   FSC® C018072

Eriu is an imprint of Bonnier Books UK
www.bonnierbooks.co.uk

This book is dedicated to my father Vincent, my sister Caroline and my husband Roland

MAP OF IRAN
Bernard's journey

Contents

Part Three – Freedom

Foreword

12 May 2023

It's a Friday morning and I didn't sleep a wink last night. I've been told only that Bernard has been 'extracted' from Mashhad Prison and taken to a clinic. I'm full of conflicting emotions: impatience; terror in case there's a last-minute change of plan by the Iranians; and the knowledge that I've got to keep up my hopes. Those feelings, despite the exhaustion of the past months, are keeping me going and helping me stay alert while I'm forced to be patient.

I get an early call from the French Foreign Affairs Crisis Centre. Bernard will be leaving Iran sometime today! Everything is ready, but they won't be able to confirm that he is actually on his way until the plane has left Iranian airspace. A little later I get another call, repeating the information and asking me not to share the news just yet.

Tension is ratcheting up inside me. I decide not to cancel my appointment with my therapist. When we're face to face, I explain what's happening and ask whether – contrary to normal practice – I can leave my phone on in case more calls come through. It's a useful session: it helps me keep my impatience under control.

I go to my barber, Florian, for a haircut. He has followed the whole story from the beginning. When the appointment is over, I step onto the street and suddenly everything starts to speed up. I'm on the pavement, just outside Rambuteau Pharmacy, when the Crisis Centre calls again. Bernard's plane is taxiing on the runway in Mashhad as it prepares to take off for Paris. They remind me that it's not over yet: while the aircraft remains in Iranian airspace, it could still be diverted by the authorities. But he's on his way. I rush in and share the news with the pharmacy staff, who know me well, and they jump for joy.

Then I get the confirmation: Bernard has left Iran!

Now begins another wait, one that slows time. Calls and messages come in from loved ones, who have learned the news from the media because it has leaked. Finally, the Crisis Centre rings to say that everything is on course and the plane should land around 7 p.m. this evening. There will be a meeting at the ministry at 6 p.m. Full of joy and impatience, I occupy myself as best I can while the minutes drag by, seeming as long as days.

I reach the ministry at 5 p.m. and am received as usual by one of the heads of the CDCS (Centre de Crise et de Soutien, the Crisis Unit within the French foreign ministry), Claudine (everyone is a head of something here). I'm given a badge that gets me into their offices. All the staff are dressed casually and everyone is happy. I'm greeted by the director, Monsieur Romatet, and another section head, Françoise.

All previous tensions between us have now evaporated: these people, with whom I've sometimes had difficult relationships, seem friendly and sincere today. The director offers me coffee, and I accept, even though I don't need stimulants and have been loaded with Xanax for months. It relaxes me, but we're going to have to wait an hour and a half for the taxi that will take us to Le Bourget Airport.

Meanwhile, Bernard's plane is advancing; we watch its progress on the monitor and attempt polite conversation.

Bernard's sister Caroline is supposed to be here, but she's late. I'm beginning to worry, but then I get a message: she's waiting outside because she thinks there are journalists inside the ministry building. (Later we realise that there were no journalists – just our anxiety!)

I go outside with Claudine to find Caroline and we get into one of the taxis. It's a big vehicle and we can't see much from the inside. Caroline and I can't stop grinning at one another, but we don't speak. For the past seven months we've talked on the phone for at least an hour every day, but now this moment has finally arrived, we're both lost for words. Claudine is in high spirits: she complains about the driver, saying he's driving badly. She tells us that she's about to be sent to Mali as a consul and has just completed military training so that she'll be able to defend herself if she's assaulted or taken hostage.

After avoiding the waiting journalists at the airport, we enter the VIP area. It feels like a miniature festival in Cannes, with cars and taxis dropping off the two of us and various ministry staff. In the semi-luxurious corporate-style lobby we're greeted by casually dressed hostesses and hosts. They lead us up to a vast first-floor lounge with large windows overlooking the runways: we're going to have the privilege of seeing Bernard's plane land.

The imposing refreshment buffet offers only soft drinks. We could have used a little Irish whiskey or at the very least some sparkling wine to celebrate this moment. But the staff confirm that there's no alcohol. I'm disappointed: it's a threadbare offering, rather as if Bernard's and Benjamin Brière's return has emptied the state coffers.

We wait a few long minutes before a tiny plane appears in the sky. It is 7 p.m. Bernard is almost home, after more than seven months of separation, anguish, and depression.

The French ministry staff are milling around in their fine clothes, maintaining their professional posture while expressing their compassion for us. The Irish officials always seem warmer and more authentic to me.

Caroline and I, glued to the window, cheer and applaud as the plane finally hits French tarmac. Then it rolls out of sight into a parking area and we are ushered downstairs to meet it.

The door of the jet opens, the pilot descends, and then Bernard is in the doorway. He is smiling. We shout with joy. The emotion is shared by all those present. This is the culmination of everyone's work, theirs and ours.

I approach Bernard, arms open, feeling true happiness, the greatest of my life.

We embrace, and he says to me, 'If you knew, if you knew . . .'

I cry then. That split second when you make contact again with your loved one – it's an emotion I've never felt before. The huge relief of it.

After giving us time for our reunion, taking photos of Bernard with me, Bernard with Caroline, Bernard with his fellow hostage, Benjamin, it's now time for formal congratulations from the officials of state. But this bit is over very quickly because, apart from the ministry staff, no one from the government has bothered to turn up – neither the President of the Republic nor any of his ministers. I ask a ministerial advisor what time his boss will arrive to mark this important day, on which France has won a victory against an authoritarian state. He replies that Madame the Minister is currently in Sweden.

'And there are no phones in Stockholm?'

His only response is to look at his feet. So much for diplomacy!

But the page has been turned. Bernard and I are ushered into an ambulance. We are heading towards the Bégin Hospital, the place where a slow and difficult reconstruction will begin – for both of us.

Roland Bonello
Paris, April 2024

Background Notes

Iran's judicial system consists of both formal and informal elements. The formal system includes courts with judges trained in Islamic law, while the informal system, known as 'Sharia courts', operates in parallel and deals with matters such as family law and disputes within religious communities. Both systems are based on Islamic principles, with the formal system having a hierarchical structure, including the Supreme Court and specialised courts, while the informal system relies more on local religious leaders and traditions.

The **Islamic Revolutionary Guard Corps (IRGC)** does not have a direct role in judicial decision-making within the official judiciary system in Iran. However, while the IRGC is not officially part of the judiciary, its members may have connections or influence within the legal system, which can indirectly affect official judicial decisions. More important, the IRGC has its own parallel judicial system, which operates independently of the official judiciary. These IRGC courts primarily handle cases related to security offences and matters concerning the IRGC's own interests. This was where I was sentenced.

Police
In Iran, the police and armed forces each have their own distinct structures:

The **Law Enforcement Force** (LEF) is responsible for maintaining internal security, enforcing laws, and ensuring public order. It is headed by a chief commander, appointed by the Supreme Leader, who holds the highest rank in the LEF. The LEF is organised into various departments, including traffic police, criminal investigation, cyber police, and special units for counter-terrorism and riot control. The LEF operates at national, provincial and local levels, with police stations and precincts across the country.

Iran's **armed forces** consist of several branches, including the Army, the Islamic Revolutionary Guard Corps, and the Law Enforcement Force. The **Iranian Army** is the conventional military force responsible for defending the country's borders and maintaining national sovereignty. The **Islamic Revolutionary Guard Corps** (IRGC) is a separate branch established after the 1979 Iranian Revolution. It operates independently of the regular military and is tasked with safeguarding the Islamic Republic's ideology and interests, both domestically and abroad. The IRGC includes ground forces, navy, air force, intelligence services, and a paramilitary force called the Basij, which operates as a volunteer militia.

The IRGC reports directly to the Supreme Leader of Iran and has significant influence in various aspects of Iranian society, including politics, economy and security. Also known as the **Guardians of the Revolution,** its primary role is to protect the Islamic Republic's ideals and regime, as well as to safeguard against internal dissent and external threats. The IRGC oversees Iran's ballistic missile programme, supports proxy groups in the region, and maintains a strong presence in domestic affairs, often suppressing dissent and enforcing ideological conformity. Economically, the IRGC controls a vast network of businesses, granting the Guardians substantial economic power and influence. Despite facing international criticism for its involvement in regional conflicts and human rights abuses, the IRGC remains a cornerstone of Iran's regime, ensuring its stability and defending its interests at home and abroad.

The armed forces also have their own chiefs of staff, with the head of the IRGC having a high-ranking position within the military hierarchy.

Overall, while both the police and armed forces play crucial roles in maintaining security and defending Iran, they operate under separate chains of command and have distinct responsibilities.

Religion: the Shia–Sunni Split

Iranian Muslims are predominantly Shia, also known as Shiite. The difference between Shiism and Sunnism goes back to the death of the Prophet.

The Prophet Muhammad was born around 570 CE, i.e. 570 years after the birth of Christ. In Islam, Christ was a prophet who came before Muhammad, but is not the Son of God. In the hours after the Prophet Muhammad died, in 632 CE, a tribal dispute broke out over who should be the Prophet's successor. Ali was one of the candidates.

This dispute festered until Ali's son, Hussein, was killed in 680 CE, during a battle in Kerbala in present-day Iraq. Islam then split into Sunni Islam (centred on Mecca, in Saudi Arabia) and Shia Islam (centred on Iran). There are many more Sunni Muslims than Shia Muslims in the world today.

Over the centuries, various ideological differences have developed between Sunni and Shia Muslims. From the Shia point of view, this schism was a 'reformation', just as Protestants broke away from Catholicism many centuries later. Most observers agree that the doctrinal differences between Sunni Muslims and Shia Muslims are much less significant than the doctrinal differences between Catholic Christians and Orthodox Christians, or between Catholic Christians and Protestant breakaways.

After the Sunni–Shia split, a Sunni 'clergy' (religious bureaucracy) took control of Sunni Islam, while a separate Shia 'clergy' took control of Shia Islam. In both cases, these clergies began interpreting/reinterpreting the Koran: things that the Prophet said; and things that the Prophet's companions may have said. On the Sunni side, around the 11th or 12th century AD the Sunni clergy decided that there was too much reinterpretation and rule-making going on, so they froze the interpretation of the Koran at that time. Critics say that this back-to-basics decision has locked Sunni Islam into a conservative time-warp. On the Shia side, reinterpretation by the clergy continues still. In this respect, Shia Muslims consider that they are the 'reformist' branch of Islam.

Ayatollah

The highest title in the hierarchy of the Shia clergy. Ayatollahs are considered experts on Islam. Ayatollah Ali Khamenei is the current Supreme Leader in Iran. He has authority over the government and all institutions (political, legal, military). He succeeded Ayatollah Khomeini, father of the Islamic Revolution, who returned to Iran in 1979 after a prolonged exile in Turkey, Iraq and then France.

The **President of Iran** is elected by popular vote for a four-year term. He oversees the cabinet and various ministries. While the President can influence policy and propose legislation, major decisions require the Supreme Leader's approval. President Ebrahim Raisi died on 19 May 2024 in a helicopter crash. His successor will be chosen in upcoming elections.

Language: The official language of Iran is Persian (or Farsi). It is an Indo-European language, like most European languages, including French, English and German. It was in the 7th century, during the country's conversion to Islam, that the Arabic alphabet replaced cuneiform writing.

Vakilabad Prison, also called the Central Prison of Mashhad, was opened in the late 1960s by Queen Farah Pahlavi, the wife of the last Shah. Mashhad Prison was built to the same blueprint as Marion Penitentiary in Illinois, which opened its doors in 1963. All accounts agree that the prison currently holds many more prisoners than it was designed for. Today, the prison population is reckoned to be 25,000. Reports say that due to the lack of sleeping space, prisoners are forced to sleep on the floor and even in the toilets.

Block 6-1: There are seven communal cells and two suites designated for inmates under sentence of execution. On the night before execution, prisoners are moved from the communal cells to these suites. Before sunrise the following day, the execution takes place. Political prisoners are also held in this section. The entrance door to Section 6-1 resembles that of an office without any specific signs to prevent identification of political prisoner sections.

Restricted visits: Those under restrictions could be murderers, fraudsters, smugglers, or ideological and political offenders. Their rights, including family visits, phone calls, and sometimes even access to fresh air, can be revoked, based on the judge's orders.

Executions: The execution hall is a room with dimensions of approximately 3x4 metres, containing several four-legged platforms. These platforms are situated in turn on a stepped platform approximately one metre above the ground. Execution is by hanging. It is possible to execute eight prisoners at once in this area. For executions, a group of soldiers are transferred from a garrison to the execution site to administer the process. After the execution, the soldiers return to their base and are rewarded with discretionary leave. Refusal to participate results in threat of detention and additional scrvice. Military personnel and prison staff are not involved in the executions themselves because their morale might be affected and they could be tempted to desert.

During an execution, a supervising judge and a cleric are present. The executioner, a clergyman, orders the placement of the platforms under the prisoner's feet.

Introduction

Today, 12 May 2024, is the first anniversary of my return from prison in Iran. As I sit down at my desk at home in Paris to write this introduction, I think of those I have left behind: the more than a dozen Westerners taken as political chess pieces and the Iranians detained by the regime under false pretexts or for just trying to exercise a little freedom. I am now free but many, including friends, are still in Mashhad, the Iranian prison where I spent over seven months, with no idea when the ordeal might end.

This is the story of my 222 days of incarceration as a state hostage in Iran. It began in October 2022, during what should have been a three-week trip to the country, when I was arrested in the north-eastern city of Mashhad. It was my fifth visit to Iran, a country I loved and where I had made many friends. The culture and history, as well as the modernity of Iran are amazing. When you understand that this empire stretched at one stage from Greece to northern India to Egypt, you cannot but admire this country on a historical and cultural level. The friendliness of the people is very like Ireland. They are suffering under religious domination as we did in Ireland in the 20th century, but on a different level, of course.

As a gay man, I knew how the regime treated the Iranian LGBT community, so when I was arrested and thrown into prison, I was terrified. I had no idea how long the unfurling nightmare would last or if my mental and physical health would hold up: my French cellmate, Benjamin Brière, had been incarcerated there for over two years, having been sentenced to eight years' imprisonment.

I knew that the justice system in Iran was a charade: the authorities could make up any charges they wanted against me and ensure that they stuck. Inside the confines of the prison, they could torture me and no one would know. Nobody could rescue me. I hoped that, because state hostages like me are valuable merchandise in complex multinational transactions, I might escape physical harm, but I knew I would not escape the notorious psychological techniques used by the Iranian security system.

How would I survive? I couldn't hide anything from my interrogators because they had seized my phone and laptop. They could inform other prisoners that I was gay. I tried not to imagine the consequences if they did this.

My health wasn't great: I have a heart condition and I am HIV positive. I would soon run out of medication; how would my body react to a sudden withdrawal of prescription drugs? I had been taking antidepressants for years; without them, would I break down completely? And what if there was another Covid crisis? The death toll in Iran during the pandemic was huge, up to a quarter of a million people, a total that was hidden from its citizens.

I also thought about those who loved me. What about my husband, Roland, back in Paris, unaware of what was happening to me? And my family? My father was expecting me at his 97th birthday party in Dublin the following month. He lived alone with a carer. (Like me, my sister Caroline lives in France.) We lost my younger brother

Declan tragically in 2006, and the prospect for them of losing another son and brother would be catastrophic. If I was held captive for years, would my father still be alive when I got out?

I have never written a book before. But I need to tell the story of what it's like to be a pawn in the Iranian hostage game – a game the West thinks it understands and knows how to play. Throughout the crisis that enveloped us, representatives of France and Ireland told me and my family to keep quiet because we might upset the Iranians. Why should we keep quiet? We *needed* to upset the Iranians.

I want the world to know what it's like for a westerner to be inside an Iranian prison; how the Iranian regime survives on terror and lies. Sadly, I believe more innocent people will be picked up in the future and bartered, as I was, in their grisly human chess game. Their families need to shout at the tops of their voices about loved ones who languish in captivity in one of the world's most repressive states, with a level of executions second only to China's.

I implore society to learn from former hostages how it can best help hostages and their families, both during imprisonment and after their return home. Currently, there is nothing in place when we return. We have to fend for ourselves to rebuild our lives, fighting for some sort of recognition. It comes as a further, cruel injustice. After the suffering we endured in Iran, now the suffering is of a new kind – sleep shattered by nightmares, sudden tears in the street, a TV news report that sparks convulsive terror – but it's a continued prison sentence all the same.

When I was in prison, I kept a diary, a detailed record of everything I was experiencing. I didn't use a pen and paper: instead, I used to dictate notes in French, via phone calls to the French embassy, to Sylvie, a good friend in southern France. The notes were in abbreviations and code. For example '2DR' (2 in Death Row) meant that there were two prisoners in cells to be executed the following morning after prayers. I knew that I would not be able to take anything out with me when – if – I was released. What follows is my moment-to-moment recollection of the events of those long months. Reconstructing my diary, I felt in some way as if I were reliving my ordeal in the present tense.

Writing onwards about my initial arrest and interrogation, then on from the day that I had real hope of release, I was able to reconstruct my memories via a more reflective lens, which has come through in my retelling. From this point in the text, the diary-style entries give way to a past-tense narration of events, still marked by when and where they occurred but from a less immediate perspective.

Part One

Chapter 1

Arrest

As I lie in my cold bed this winter evening in Mashhad central prison, I can remember almost every detail of the evening of my arrest on Monday 3 October 2022. My friend Mike and I had walked around the perimeter of the Imam Reza shrine complex in Mashhad, the second-biggest city in Iran, admiring the beautifully lit golden domes and minarets, with Mike taking a steady stream of photos on his Canon camera. At around five o'clock every evening, the multicoloured lights of the complex are illuminated, and large crowds of the faithful begin to gather for evening prayer. The holy shrine is the burial place of the prophet Iman Reza, which lies within the largest mosque in the world, a vast complex of courtyards, mosques, museums and libraries.

Mike's given name is Abolfazl, but he prefers Mike. As a Shia Muslim, albeit non-practising, Mike was able to get closer to the shrine than me without having to enter the site itself to take more photographs. As I watched from the railings at the entrance, it was pleasant to reflect on our journey so far. We had been on the go since my arrival in Iran on 17 September, never spending more than one night in each place we visited. I had first got in touch with

Mike in 2017 after a week's trek in the Central Desert with his agency, Adventure Iran. I work as a tourism consultant and when I got back to France, I contacted him to offer help in marketing his agency's tours in Europe. Having previously worked for the Irish Tourist Board in Paris, I had plenty of experience selling a 'difficult' destination, as Ireland was during the 1970s and 1980s because of the Troubles. Mike was keen to collaborate, so over the next four years I visited Iran almost once a year. This trip marked my fifth visit; we were working together on a project to develop a rail version of the Silk Road, which had passed through the city of Mashhad.

When Mike had taken enough photos of the beautifully lit complex, we left the shrine to find some food, heading across a paved square dotted with trees. As we passed a traffic-police kiosk, two men approached us. One was tall and fat with glasses, dressed in cheap, casual clothes; the other was small and wore a well-cut jacket. As they strode over, I couldn't help but immediately see the two as the comedy duo Laurel and Hardy.

I have gone over the following events in my mind countless times since arriving in prison.

The small man pulled out an ID card and asked us to follow him. As we went with them, Mike whispered to me that they were from a state security organisation. I was a little nervous because this was the first time in all my visits to Iran that I had been stopped by the authorities. I wasn't concerned at first, being used to the violence and ferocity of French protests, but as we followed the men, I felt a creeping sense of anxiety: with the recent protests over the death of Jina Mahsa Amini in the custody of the morality police, Mike with his bulky camera and so few foreign tourists in Mashhad, we were bound to attract attention.

We stopped beside some trees away from the main bustle of the streets, and the men asked us to sit down on a low wall. They began asking Mike questions about his camera and why he was taking photographs. The big one, Hardy, sat beside Mike while Laurel made calls on his small Nokia-like phone. We were asked for our identity documents, and I gave them my Irish and French passports. Mike gave them his Iranian identity card.

Laurel, the little guy in the jacket, moved away a short distance to talk on his phone while holding the passports and Mike's identity card. In the meantime, Mike was talking to Hardy. The two had been polite and friendly, as had nearly always been the case when we spoke with officials in Iran. I imagined that we would be on our way in a few minutes, once they saw that we were harmless tourists. Nonetheless, I assumed that they were armed.

After a few minutes, Laurel came back and asked for our phones. Then he disappeared with them. For the first time, Mike looked really worried. We waited without talking. A few people out for an evening stroll passed by, but they seemed to be avoiding looking in our direction.

I was now beginning to feel more concerned. There was a lot of information on my phone that I preferred the authorities not to find. I had nothing to hide, but my private life was on my phone and there was no way of preventing the security forces from accessing it. Crucially, there were no photos of the demonstration we had seen in Tabriz in the north-west of the country, which I was relieved about because these might be seen as supporting the protest movement. But there were photos taken of a burnt-out mosque in Rasht, on the Caspian Sea, a photo of two policemen taken from our hotel room in Tabriz, as well as a short clip taken in Tabriz, just before Mike and I saw the protestors. To make matters worse, we had no way of telling which faction of authorities these were; were they with the security police or the Revolutionary Guards? If it was the latter, we were in trouble. This group were under the direct control of the Supreme Leader Ali Khamenei and were reputed to be brutally crushing the current protest movement.

After about twenty minutes, Laurel reappeared with two other men. One was big, wearing a surgical mask and glasses, well dressed. Although polite, he refused to give me his name, so he was assigned the name of George in my mind. He had a younger sidekick, who wore a black mask which covered from the base of his neck to just under his nose, trendy runners, black jeans and a black jacket. Both men kept patting their jackets, and it struck me that they were probably armed; but because I live in France, where all the police are armed, that did not particularly worry me.

George spoke French and English. He asked me what I was doing in Mashhad. I explained that we had wanted to visit the shrine because it was one of Iran's most famous sites. I told him it was my fifth visit to the country and that, with Mike, I had visited the northern provinces, from the Turkish border to Mashhad. He asked for the codes to our phones, which we gave him. I imagined that if I refused, they would put pressure on Mike to get me to give them my codes. On top of which, I thought, the Iranian security services probably had the technology to hack my phone and computer.

George walked away from us, talking on his phone. He had a smartphone too, but I think he was using his personal phone. After some time, he returned and asked me if I had taken pictures of demonstrations. I said I hadn't. I could see that the sidekick had pulled down his mask and opened his jacket. Tucked into an inside pocket was a clear plastic bag containing black plastic ties. I felt my stomach lurch.

George went away again for a while before returning without our phones but holding our identity documents. He said that they needed to talk to us for a bit longer in a place nearby. He told me not to be concerned; it wouldn't take long. I had no choice but to comply. The six of us set off on foot down the steps from the square towards a street lined with a caravanserai (roadside travellers' inns dating back to the Silk Road period). We walked for about five minutes without talking as I wondered what to do. Should I ask them to allow me to contact the Irish and French embassies? Or maybe we were going somewhere to complete paperwork which could not be done in the street? Maybe then they would realise that I was in the country to promote it, not to undermine it.

George opened the door to a modern building. We climbed the stairs to the first floor, passing a man coming down with a tray of tea who said 'Salaam' (the standard greeting in Iran). We were told to remove our shoes before entering a large room covered with green prayer mats. The room was lined with bookshelves, photos of Ayatollah Khomeini and the present Supreme Leader, Ali Khamenei, as well as framed texts from the Koran.

Everyone except the trendy sidekick entered, all in stockinged feet. I started to look at the books, but Mike urged me to sit down on one of the chairs that lined the wall. He looked very nervous and downcast. George sat down behind a desk while Hardy sat with us. Laurel spent most of the time talking on his phone as he paced the room. There was a clock on the wall, and I saw that it was now around 9 p.m. We had already been in detention for about three hours. I still felt hopeful that this was all going to end shortly and that we would be able to go for a meal before returning to Mike's father's flat where we had arranged to stay the night.

Then George asked me to leave the room and wait in the stairwell. The sidekick went with me and watched me as I sat on a step. It was warm and stuffy; there were no open windows. I could not hear any noise from the street. The door to the main room was ajar, and I could hear Mike answering George's questions calmly in Persian. Then we swapped places, Mike shooting me an anxious look when we passed in the stairwell. He stood outside while I was questioned. In French, George told me not to be afraid: everything would be sorted out shortly. He quizzed me about my previous four visits to Iran, about my work, and my family and relatives in France and in Ireland. He asked me what I thought of Iran. I explained that I was an enthusiastic admirer of his country and enjoyed meeting Iranians. However, I thought to myself that, with these personal questions being asked of me, rather than questions about my trip, things were not looking great. There was perhaps less chance of us being released soon.

Mike was called in again and I was relegated to the stairwell once more. I asked the sidekick if I could go to the toilet and he took me to one in the basement.

Everything was clean and modern. All I could detect was the smell of cleaning fluid. I glimpsed some other men waiting at the entrance to the building. When I returned, the sidekick offered me tea, which I accepted, but I was also getting hungry. There was no offer of food.

Next, I was questioned alone about photographs they had found on my iPhone. A man, whom I hadn't seen before, walked into the book-lined room carrying my Mac and iPad. I realised that this meant that our captors had been to Mike's father's flat and had searched it. So things were getting serious. Where was this going to end?

I was taken from the interview room again and Mike went back in, this time for a longer session. Then it was my turn once more. Finally, George told me that they would have to take us both to another place. I was scared now and in a cold sweat. What was going to happen to me?

A man came into the room holding a black bag, from which he took a camera and set it up to photograph us. I was asked to give him my name, date of birth and home address. The man then pulled out some forms and an ink pad and proceeded to take my fingerprints. I was asked to hand over everything in my pockets. George and another man examined everything and filled in a form. George noted my Visa, American Express and Iranian card numbers and listed the cash, about €700 and some rials, the Iranian currency. I was asked to sit on one of the chairs along the wall while they did the same to Mike.

We could not talk because he was seated on the far side of the room. I sat there looking over at my good friend with a certain amount of resentment as my mind raced. Why did he have to photograph the mosque with a camera that was so large it made us stand out so much? If we had just strolled around the city innocuously, perhaps we wouldn't have been picked up. Had we been followed since our arrival in Mashhad, or only on that evening? Why hadn't Mike been able to talk us out of the situation, the way he had done on previous visits? I shivered despite the warmth of the stuffy room. Then everyone left except Laurel and Hardy.

George came back with his sidekick, who was no longer wearing his jacket. He said that we were going to be driven to another location. Mike was told to go downstairs first. They told me I would join him shortly. I was kept back for a moment before being taken to put on my shoes in the stairwell. I never imagined that I wouldn't see Mike again.

When I got outside there was no sign of my friend, just an old Peugeot with two unfamiliar men in the front. I was put into the back on my own. The doors either side of me were locked before we set off. My heart was pounding. I had lost my last familiar contact, and I was now completely alone, with no way of contacting anyone. When he'd said that everything was going to be okay, George had lied to me.

Chapter 2

Detention

The car moved slowly through endless narrow lanes and streets. I was uneasy but still somewhat blasé about the situation: I had been in more dangerous places before, such as the border between Uganda and Rwanda, where I was stopped on a desolate road by a young man with a machine gun and a big knife. Here, I knew that I wasn't in any physical danger. As we drove along, I was surprised to see all the women's clothes shops with so much lingerie on display. I had noticed this before in big Iranian cities, like Shiraz, Tabriz and Isfahan, but never on the scale visible here. Despite Mashhad's reputation as one of the most conservative cities in the country, I knew that, for Shia Muslims, it was also the prostitution capital of Central Asia and the Middle East. Prostitution in Mashhad is institutionalised and simple: a man simply goes to a cleric and gets 'married' for a day to the woman he wants to spend time with. The juxtaposition of religion and vice really captures the way Mashhad operates.

As we drove, I thought of my husband back in France. Roland said he would never visit the city after reading *The Spider of Mashhad* by Mana Neyestani, a graphic novel based on the true story of Saeed Hanaei, a fervently religious serial killer in the early 2000s. Neyestani captures the level of conservatism of the population of Mashhad through their intolerance of the sex workers murdered by the serial killer. A significant section of society actually protested in defence of the killer since his actions were seen as righteous.

My Irish Catholic upbringing and education made me an early atheist and profoundly humanist. From the age of four, I was educated by the De La Salle Brothers, and I was beaten from the beginning, usually by the maths and Irish teachers, because they were two subjects I was not good at. I was sometimes dragged by the ear to another, lower class to be humiliated in front of the pupils. This continued to the end of secondary school. At the age of seventeen, a few months before going to university, I was beaten by the headmaster with his leather strap (there was a metal strip sewn into it) for not hanging my anorak in the college cloakroom.

But despite my misgivings about organised religion, Iranian culture in general was something Roland and I embraced wholeheartedly. A clinical psychologist working with children, Roland is as keen a traveller as I am. In 2020, we travelled to Iran, as we had done before, this time to try to develop a tour that would offer visitors more contact with the local people and culture. One idea was a cooking tour in which participants would be paired with a local Iranian woman so they could learn a traditional recipe. They would go to the market together, then return to her home to cook with her and to eat the meal. Our research took us off the beaten tourist track, and we met lots of women who told us about how complicated life in Iran was for them. I am not sure if people in the West realise how difficult day-to-day life is for many Iranian women: for example, requiring the permission of their husband to work or to travel abroad. They can study law but can never become a judge. In 2012, universities banned women from almost 80 degree courses. The list included engineering, nuclear physics, computer science, archaeology and business. In the end, the cooking tours were put on hold because of the Covid crisis.

All these thoughts were running through my head as we drove. After some time, the man in the passenger seat handed me a blindfold and told me to put it on. I felt as if I was in a spy film when the main character – me in this case – gets caught. It was the first time in my life someone had told me to put on a blindfold. The man then made sure it was pulled down properly so that I could see nothing. Every other sense was instantly heightened. I could hear the noise of people and traffic. We drove on for another twenty minutes. I was counting those minutes in my head.

Finally, the car slowed down and I could hear a gate being opened. Then voices. The car door opened and I was helped out. I could feel gravel under my shoes. I heard my name being spoken: 'Phelan, Bernard. Father, Vincent'. This, as I was to discover, was how Iranian prisoners were identified because there were too many people with the same name.

The driver took me into a building and the blindfold was removed. I was dazzled by the very brightly lit, windowless room. The place was modern and clean. On the walls were the usual pictures of the Supreme Leader, Khamenei, and the President, Ebrahim Raisi.

The driver gave a wad of papers to the man sitting behind the desk. They got me to use my fingerprint to 'sign' a pile of forms. I did not resist because there was no point in making things worse. They took away my shoes and belt. I was brought down a corridor and a cell door was opened. They gave me a blanket. Then the metal door clanged shut behind me. It was a large room and, in a corner, sitting on the floor, was a young man dressed in jeans and a white shirt. As I walked towards him to speak to him, the door opened again and guards, wearing Covid medical masks, told me in English to come back out. I was taken to another, much smaller cell, in which two men were sitting on the floor. I'm not sure why I was moved again so soon. Once inside the new cell, I made a beeline for the toilet, which was concealed behind a low wall with a door set into it. There was a sink in the corner where I could wash.

Afterwards, I greeted the two men sharing my cell. They both looked up but did not smile. They were Iranian. One spoke English and worked in telecommunications. The other man, I was told, was a student but he did not speak English. When I asked why they had been detained, they both raised their clenched fists in the air: they were protestors, therefore hostile to the regime.

Suddenly the door opened again and the two Iranians were taken away. I wondered whether the guards had heard us and didn't like us talking in English. I was left alone in the cell, which was about four metres square. There was a small window high up to the right of the door. After a while, the bottom of two flaps in the cell door opened and a tray of food was handed in with a cup of tea and a small bottle of mineral water. I was very hungry and wolfed down the rice and tepid stew.

It must have been very late; I was exhausted both physically and mentally. With no bed or mattress in the cell, I curled up on the floor, pulled the blanket over my head and tried to sleep. The ventilation system, which sounded like an old washing machine at its noisiest cycle, and the powerful overhead lighting, seemed to completely penetrate my senses. I could not sleep. There was a CCTV camera in the corner. These cameras were to become part of my life for the foreseeable future.

In the night, I heard voices in the corridor outside and the sudden clank of a cell door opening. There was shouting, followed by the sound of a man being beaten with something. A stick, or maybe a truncheon? Every few seconds he screamed. A deep male voice shouted in response and there were grunts as the blows continued. I pressed my hands against my ears to try to block out the sound, but it was no good: the shouts and screams filled my head. Was it one of the men who had been taken from my cell? I was living a nightmare. What was going to happen to me?

The loudspeaker in the cell began to broadcast the call to prayer, which lasted about five minutes. So, I thought, it must be very early in the morning. I hadn't slept. I kept thinking I was in a bad dream and that I would wake up back home in Paris. Or that the authorities had made a terrible mistake and would come in at any moment to apologise and set me free. How was I going to contact my family and friends? Roland and my family would be worried if I didn't manage to get my flight home in a week's time. They might already be concerned that they hadn't heard from me for about five days, but then I reasoned that because of state interference, the internet is very patchy in Iran, and they might assume it was simply a communications problem. Maybe they would worry that

31

I'd had a car accident: Iran has one of the world's worst road fatality rates. And what about my medication? I take six different drugs every day: some are essential to keep me in good health. On arrival at the detention centre, I had enough to last the final few days I'd been expecting to stay in Iran. After that, I knew I would be at serious risk. What worried me most was no longer having the medication that would reduce the risk of a stroke and depression. I had had a serious breakdown about ten years before, which had put me in hospital for three months. With these thoughts spinning in my mind, I pulled the blanket over my head again and tried to sleep.

Chapter 3

Nothing to Hide

I must have slept eventually that night, because the next thing I remember was a knock on the door and the bottom hatch opening to reveal a plastic cup of tea, bread and cheese. When I'd eaten, I washed as best I could in the basin; there was no hot water, soap or toothbrush.

Later, the bottom hatch opened again and I was handed a blindfold to put on. Then I was told to put my hands out through the hatch to be handcuffed. With my blindfold in place, I heard the door open and a hand on my shoulder pushed me along a corridor and into what seemed like a room. I was put into a seat and told in French to take off the blindfold. The handcuffs were then removed.

In front of me, smiling, was George. He said, in French, that I was not to worry: everything would be sorted out very soon. I managed a laugh and said that, so far, everything that had happened had made me think the opposite. A camera on a tripod to George's left was filming our exchange. High up on one of the walls behind my interrogator was a small window revealing a rectangle of blue sky.

George asked for the passwords to my laptop and iPad. I gave them to him. I figured that not cooperating wouldn't help my situation. And I felt that I had nothing apart from my personal life to hide.

He asked me about my earlier travels in Iran: where I'd been, whom I'd met, what I'd seen. I decided to tell the truth. It would be too complicated to lie and, anyway, they had access to everything on my computer and phone. The only thing that concerned me was getting my Iranian friends into trouble.

First, I told George that Mike and I had got caught in a demonstration in Tabriz. Coming out of the huge bazaar – a UNESCO site and an important destination on the Silk Road route – after lunch, Mike and I had found large groups of people standing around. There was a smell of tear gas and we could hear in the distance the sound of shouting and car horns beeping. Some shopkeepers were pulling down their metal shutters. We collected our belongings and headed to Jomhouri Eslami Street, a big avenue that bisects the city, to get a taxi. We did not get far because the demonstrators were confronting the security services there. There was a footbridge over this road and youths were throwing projectiles at the security personnel below. I heard gunshots in the distance.

I took a video on my phone with the camera facing the ground as we walked back to the tourist office. I knew that this might be problematic if I was caught, but I was curious and wanted to show my friends at home what was going on. We waited in the doorway of the office, watching the demonstrators moving along, followed by security people, some on motorbikes. The director of the tourist office said that there was an underground station nearby and gave us directions. There were stones all over Jomhouri Eslami Street. We could see the demonstrators further up the street being pursued by the security services. There was nobody in uniform and no police cars, just unmarked cars and men on motorbikes, their number plates covered, all armed.

Mike and I dashed across the street and headed south to reach the underground station. At the first junction to our right, we saw youths being rounded up by plain-clothes police on motorbikes. There were sometimes up to three men on each bike! It was tempting but too risky to take a photograph. We waited a bit for the crowd to move on.

We continued along the shop-lined street – many shops had their shutters down – and finally arrived at a big square. Shahid Mohaqqeqi underground station was situated at the far end. There was utter chaos in front of us, with people shouting and running everywhere. A smell of smoke mixed with tear gas filled the air, accompanied now and again by the sound of a gunshot. I am not sure if the Iranian security services bothered to use rubber bullets. At the far end of the brick-strewn square was a burning vehicle, a van or a minibus.

Mike and I decided to make a dash for the station entrance at the far side. As we were running across the square, a woman shouted to us that the underground service had been shut down. We turned around and ran back to the edge of the square and stood outside an electrical store, unsure what to do next. Suddenly the door to the shop opened, and we were invited inside. We were given seats and tea in this small shop, while people continued to run to and fro outside. The men around us carried on working: it was a wholesale business of electrical supplies. After waiting for around an hour until things quietened down, the store owner said he would take us to get a taxi. I think we must have walked for almost half an hour before arriving at a dual carriageway where the kind shop-owner was able to wave down a passing car to take us to our hotel.

At the hotel, everything was normal, but from our room on the seventh floor we could see and hear the odd shot. Suddenly I noticed what looked like riot police driving into the hotel car park below our window and parking their cars. There was writing on the backs of their jackets but I could not make out the wording. I took some photos in the dark of two policemen in the street below.

As I recounted this tale to George, I stressed to him that I had taken no photographs of the demonstrators or the security services who were present at the actual protest. He made no comment, simply making notes.

The next contentious photo on my device had been taken in Orumiyeh, a city about 150 kilometres west of Tabriz. We were in a fruit-juice bar when suddenly men, in army jackets, wearing helmets and holding sticks, started to march down the street, directed by non-uniformed men. Some of these young men were wearing jeans or tracksuit bottoms and sneakers. They also wore scarves over their mouths or Covid masks, so that, I imagine, they could not be recognised. They stopped, spaced out along the street. I was able to take a photograph from just inside the doorway. We guessed that a demonstration had been planned and this was to be the welcoming committee. Mike and I crossed in front of these men to get to our hotel across the street. Later that evening, when we went out to eat, there was no sign of the young men or the remains of the demonstration.

Finally, there were some photos from a night we had stayed in the city of Gonbad-e Qabus, about 500 kilometres north-east of Tehran. We'd stopped for something to drink beside the city's famous landmark: a tower, 61 metres high, which dates back to AD 1007. A huge mustard-coloured building with a conical roof, it contains the remains of the ruler Qabus. Outside the entrance to the park surrounding the tower were a few motorbikes, exactly like the ones I had seen used by the security services in Tabriz. Again, the number plates had been covered by black metal plates. As we walked back to our car, I had taken some photographs of the bikes.

George then began to question me about my private life. 'Are you married?' he asked.

'I am,' I replied.

'What's your wife's name?'

I said, 'Roland Bonello', not specifying Roland's gender.

George looked at me sharply. 'That's a man's name.'

'Yes. Same-sex marriage is allowed in most European countries,' I said, hoping that this gave him the answer he was looking for.

'Do you have children?'

'No.'

'Why haven't you adopted one?'

'Oh, I'm too old,' I replied. A discussion ensued about the ideal age to have children.

Afterwards I was taken, blindfolded and handcuffed, back to my cell. I was frightened, but I could do nothing about it, so, out of boredom, I climbed on the low wall that surrounded the toilet to see if I could glimpse anything out of the high window. This caused an uproar, with the guards, who'd seen me on the cell's CCTV, coming to the hatch, masked, and gesturing for me to get down.

Later, I started to fiddle discreetly with the hinges of a low door that separated the toilet from the rest of the cell. I threw the screws down the toilet. Knowing that the next visitor was going to be in for a bit of a surprise and the authorities would have 'fun' repairing the door made me smile: I am of a provocative nature when put under pressure.

After a while, a guard came to the hatch with my laptop. He said that the password I had given was not working. I typed it directly through the hatch to show him that I was not lying. He went off but came back a few minutes later to say that it was still not working. He passed me a mobile phone. George was at the other end of the line. 'Look,' I said, 'I've given you the correct password each time, and if you are incapable of accessing my Mac, it's not my fault. I'll unlock the computer one more time and after that, you can get lost.' I knew that I was taking a risk being this brusque with them, but it worked. They did not bother me about it any more.

I was taken out of my cell again but this time, when the blindfold was removed, I found myself in a small, carpeted room. A man was sitting behind a desk with an open ledger in front of him. To his left, three men were sitting, with George, again smiling, in the middle. A fifth man in a bright blue suit sat with a notebook open on the desk. They were all in their stockinged feet, as was I.

George explained that the man with the ledger was a judge and that my arrest was to be formalised.

'I want to speak to my embassy,' I insisted. 'I'm not signing anything.'

Still with a smile on his face, George said, 'So, you're not cooperating then.'

I lost my temper. 'Look, your idiot colleagues were unable to unlock my computer with the correct password, which I've given you more than once!' The others asked George to translate what I'd said. He did so and they shrugged. The oldest man in the room, smiling a little, offered me a bottle of water. After further discussion, a document was put in front of me and I was handed a pen. They stared at me, expectantly, waiting for me to sign. I folded my arms, shook my head, and said nothing. I'd started to sweat – I wasn't sure whether it was from fear or the stuffiness of the room.

'Look,' George said. 'Things will get worse for you if you refuse to sign.'

'Things are already pretty bad,' I replied.

After about an hour, they gave up and I was escorted, blindfolded and handcuffed, back to my cell.

Chapter 4

'Do Not Worry'

It was hard to gauge the time passing, but I guessed that a day had gone by at this stage. As it got dark outside, I heard a large vehicle with a diesel engine enter the compound. It appeared to manoeuvre, then stop, but the engine was still running. After a long interval, I heard footsteps outside the door of my cell and a guard pushed a blindfold through the bottom hatch. When I put my hands through for the handcuffs, black plastic ties were put on my wrists. I was taken out and along a corridor. There were lots of voices and movement around me. Someone was holding on to my shoulder. My name was called and my blindfold was removed. I was made to fingerprint a form and given back my boots and belt, before the blindfold was put back on, as well as a new pair of handcuffs. A door was opened and cooler air hit my face for a moment before I was put into the vehicle I must have heard earlier. It was a coach or a minibus, I guessed. I was ushered down the aisle and put in an inside seat with a guard next to me. He had what seemed like an electronic gadget that played prerecorded messages in English with a strange 'tinny' sound, like a robot talking in a 1980s' film. He held it to my ear and I heard, 'Do not worry. All will be all right soon,' and, 'We are here to look after you.' I laughed nervously.

I could hear sounds and vibrations as more people came on board. No one spoke. The smell of diesel filled the vehicle. We drove over what felt like gravel and across a bump onto a road, then drove for about half an hour until the vehicle slowed down and the engine was turned off. A guard took me off the minibus; we walked a few metres and entered what seemed to be a building. My blindfold was removed, and the plastic ties cut. I was in a small holding room with three or four guards. My name was called and I put my fingerprint on another form.

I was taken to a small room, which appeared to be a place for detainee–family meetings, because of the one-way mirror and the phone handset on a shelf. I could see my reflection in the mirror and I wondered who was on the other side. I was given a blue jacket, a matching pair of trousers and a pair of flip-flops. I changed and handed my clothes through the door. The blindfold and handcuffs were put back on. So I was now in a prison uniform. I was too tired to reflect on this new step into incarceration but it did feel strange.

I was taken out and along a corridor with a gentle upward slope. I heard a metal door opening and was pushed over a step. The door slammed shut behind me. Silence. Then I heard the lower hatch opening. Once again, I removed the blindfold and handed it over and then put my hands through to have the handcuffs removed.

This cell was big and modern with a very high ceiling. There was a separate room with a toilet and a stone wash-basin. The cell was L-shaped, roughly six metres long and four metres wide. There was a camera high up on the wall with a speaker. To the left of the door was an intercom with a button. Again, there was no bed, but a pair of blue blankets were folded in a corner. In addition to the cell's very bright lighting, two large noisy extractor fans were set high up above the door.

Soon, the lower hatch opened and a tray of food and a plastic cup of tea arrived. I sat in the corner opposite the door and ate my dinner of rice and pieces of chicken. I reckoned that I had been imprisoned for a few days: it was difficult to keep track of the number and the time, even with the cell's tannoy system announcing the regular calls to prayer. I kept thinking of my family back in France and Ireland and how they were going to take the news of my arrest. Roland, before my departure, had asked me if I was sure about the trip to Iran, given the protests that were breaking out. I pointed out that this was not the first time there had been violent protests in parts of the country. He told me to be careful and that maybe I would be part of history. Little did he know.

After eating, I folded one blanket to make a mattress on the hard floor, then used the other to cover myself and try to cut out the light and noise. It was very warm and uncomfortable in the uniform and with the blankets pulled over me to shut out the light. Between the noise of the fans, the speaker with the calls to prayer and the noise of opening and closing cell doors, I got little sleep. I had no idea of the time, but when the lower hatch opened and a tray was handed in with tea, bread, jam and a plastic spoon, I guessed it must be morning. I sat in the corner eating and wondered what was going to happen next.

When the top hatch opened, a masked guard passed me a little square of soap and a small blue towel. I kept the plastic cup because it was the only way I could pour the cold water over myself to wash. Then I was given a toothbrush, onto which the guard squeezed toothpaste. I was told that I must brush my teeth straight away and give him back the toothbrush.

I had brought enough medication to last for two days after my planned return date, 10 October. From my calculations, it was now 5 October. But my remaining medication had been seized, together with my other possessions. The guards brought me my tablets from time to time. Then I had an idea. The next time the guard passed me my tablets and insisted that I swallow them in front of him, I put them under my tongue. The hatch closed and I went into the toilet, closed the door and spat the tablets into the hole in the ground that served as a toilet bowl, using the cleaning hose to wash them away. The camera in the cell could not see what I was doing. My plan was to make myself so ill from the lack of drugs that the authorities would be concerned for my well-being and cut short my detention. I knew the Iranian regime would not like to hand back a European in a worse state than when he arrived.

My plan in place, I started to pace the room to get some exercise.

Chapter 5

The Forging of a Rebel

After a bit, the lower hatch was opened and the blind-fold-and-handcuffs routine took place. I was taken into a room where I could hear people talking and was put in a chair. The handcuffs were removed and George's voice told me in French to take off the blindfold. He was sitting behind a desk. I found myself sitting in a chair with a flip-over table attached for writing – the kind I'd used as a student at University College Dublin. There was a cloth screen to my right with at least one person sitting behind it. A video camera on a tripod was running, filming the encounter.

'So, we found some material on your phone,' George said. He handed me a form with a photo I'd taken printed on it. It had been taken at a party in Tehran in 2018. 'Who are the people in this picture?' he asked.

I knew better than to give him my friends' full names, so I pointed to one or two of them and gave him their first names. He didn't comment about the fact that it was clear that we were drinking home-made wine as well as some stronger liquor. The consumption of alcohol in Iran is forbidden though very widespread. I had even seen pictures of grapes being pressed with a machine by a man in the Grand Bazaar in Tehran to obtain grape juice, from which wine could be made.

George handed me a pen. 'Put a number beside each person in the photo and list their first names underneath please.' I obeyed as best I could. 'Now, your fingerprint,' he said, indicating the ink pad beside the form, into which I pressed my index finger and marked the form. This process continued with other photos taken on my previous trips to Iran.

Sometimes, George was not happy when I could not name the person or the exact location shown in the image. 'I can't remember,' I would say. This was true – some of those gathered around the table were just fellow guests – but I also knew that the security services were trying to catch people unsympathetic to the regime. I wasn't going to help them,

'Well, try harder!' he would bark. From behind the screen someone was giving him instructions in Persian.

The interview lasted about an hour and then I was taken back to my cell. I couldn't sleep, even with a blanket over my head, and the noise of the fans was oppressive, so I just sat in the corner and tried to think of positive things, such as Roland. We had met in 2003 and married in 2014, as soon as French law permitted. We had been in a civil union since 2004, the same year I obtained French nationality. I'd been living in the country since 1986, when I came to work for the Irish Tourist Board. I also thought about how my father, who would be 97 in November, would react to my arrest and imprisonment. He tends to worry a lot and I could imagine my poor sister Caroline trying to reassure him over the phone, not an easy task because his hearing is bad. I tried to think about the house in Banyuls-sur-Mer on the Mediterranean near the Spanish border, where Roland and I had moved a short time before. We had been living in Cerbère when a friend told us about a house with plenty of ground, parts of which dated to the 12th century. Moving to Banyuls wasn't a difficult decision to make. Now, I missed nature and the wide open spaces of the Pyrenees and the feel of the tramontane wind blowing in my face. I tried to think of what I would do when I got out of this mess: write a book and get a dog now, instead of waiting for my retirement. I'd had a Labrador, Max, for about seven years a long time ago. We were very close and did lots of things together. Max would accompany me to work, visit customers and travel around France with me by train.

After a lunch of rice and stew, I was taken out of the cell, blindfolded and handcuffed once more and taken down a corridor, but after the slope, we turned right and I was guided into a room and the door closed behind me. Silence, so I removed the blindfold. I was in a sort of indoor courtyard. There was an opaque skylight above me and two potted plants in the middle, a white plastic chair along the wall to the left. The lower hatch was opened so that I could have the handcuffs removed and hand back the blindfold. I think the room was about fifteen metres long and six metres wide. The walls, like the cell, were of polished stone. I walked in circles around the room, changing direction every now and then. This treatment is common: as I was to learn, all hostages spend weeks or months like this, in solitary confinement with daily interrogations. I sat in the chair, which was great for my back after so much time on the cell floor. Were the authorities concerned about my wellbeing? By this stage, I was worried about my own sanity. Apart from the isolation, I had little idea what day it was, or even what time of day, on top of which, the bright lighting and endless noise made me wonder if I was slowly going mad. In about a quarter of an hour I was taken back to the cell.

That evening, I noticed a rash spreading over my lower chest, which I wanted desperately to scratch. Was it the uniform jacket, the blankets, the food, the water (I heard later that in these isolation blocks the authorities were able to tamper with a particular cell's water supply) or was I ill?

That evening I took off the jacket and trousers and tried to sleep in my underpants because it was too warm. Within minutes, a voice on the speaker told me to get dressed. Shortly after, the door opened and in marched three guards. I stood up in my underpants. They pointed at the jacket and trousers, indicating that I must put them back on. I showed them the rash on my chest and pointed to the jacket and rugs. They appeared to understand and they left, returning with a new uniform and new blankets. I washed and tried to go to sleep.

The following day, George started asking me about religion. I told him that I was an atheist. He appeared baffled that I did not believe in anything. I was baptised a Catholic, but from around the age of nineteen I stopped going to church. This was a topic that was to come up regularly in future discussions in the prison. The Iranians could not accept that I did not believe in an afterlife.

George next asked me about my life in Europe. I had to tell them about my family and why I had come to live in France in 1986. He asked me about my relatives and what they did. I refrained from telling them about my father's brother Andrew's involvement in the setting up of Amnesty International or about a second cousin, Alisdair, who sometimes makes controversial television documentaries for the BBC and Channel 4. But I did mention that one of my cousins in Scotland, Patricia, was married to a judge, Lord Angus Glennie. I was a bit puzzled by this line of questioning: I couldn't see why the Iranians would find this interesting, but perhaps they wanted to find out if I had any relatives working in the media or with Iranian opposition. Either way, I wondered if George would ever run out of questions to ask me.

'Look,' I said to George at one point. 'I'm going to run out of meds in a few days. I might fall very ill and you could be sending me back in a wheelchair – or a coffin.'

'I understand,' George said.

'I'm taking medication for HIV, high blood pressure, stroke, osteoporosis . . .' I listed out my medical conditions in the hope that this might put pressure on George. Instead, he simply shrugged and changed the subject. Then he began to ask me a serious of strange questions, which revealed to me the extent of his misunderstanding of the West. I'm not sure where he'd been getting his information, but he wanted to know why in Europe some people demonstrated in the nude! I pointed out that in certain European countries, such as the Netherlands and Denmark, this happened, and that there were even protests by naked cyclists. I told him it was a peaceful form of protest. He went on to talk about the Yellow Vest movement in France (les Gilets Jaunes).

'Oh,' I explained, 'they're not a significant issue any more.'

George shook his head. 'I hear that they are destabilising the French government.'

'That's rubbish!' I exclaimed. 'You couldn't possibly know what's going on in France because you don't live there.'

Unperturbed, he asked me to name my favourite film. I replied that it was *2001: A Space Odyssey*. He wanted a more recent film. I thought about the French gay film *La Cage aux Folles* but thought better of it. Instead, I said that *Jerico*, a Colombian film about women in a mountain village, was full of colour and music. He then asked me about my favourite book. I replied that it was Joyce's *Ulysses*. (I nearly said Oscar Wilde's 'The Ballad of Reading Gaol'.) He said he was reading a book that they'd taken from me, *The Forging of a Rebel* by Arturo Barea, and was finding it very interesting. I said that I had read the first two books in the trilogy, describing the author's youth and the Spanish Civil War. I told him that I was annoyed to be deprived of this, the third, which covered Barea's life after Franco seized power. George promised to give the book back to me when he'd finished it. He never did.

In my cell after lunch, I started to examine the polished stone walls to see if I could make out designs or objects. I could recognise the shape of a bird and even a pig. I realised that in the cell and toilet there was nothing sharp and no tiles that could be broken to fashion a sharp object. They did not want prisoners to hurt themselves: we were valuable material. A foreign hostage in good health, I imagined, could be kept longer and be worth more when it came to negotiations. Someone who had been kept in jail for a month must be worth less than one who had been imprisoned for a number of years.

That evening, the noise of the fans drove me mad. I called the intercom and put my hand over my ears so the guards could see me on their camera feed. Of course, none of them spoke English, so they hung up. I kept pressing the button and eventually someone came to the hatch. The guard had a smartphone with Google Translate on it and I spelled out the problem, asking him to switch off the fan. He nodded, and shortly afterwards a blissful silence fell. But it was still hard to sleep fully clothed and under the strong lights, alone in the warm, airless room.

♠　♠　♠

What I guessed to be the following day, when I entered the office, there was a different person behind the desk. Like George, he would not tell me his name, so I nick-named the new man 'Henry'. He was in his late thirties, a little on the plump side. He spoke excellent French with a good accent. I guessed he had been sent from Tehran to question me. George was there, too, with other men behind a screen to my right.

Henry wore a surgical mask and white latex gloves. I could see the hairs of his hands showing through the latex. He kept pulling the latex around his fingers. I did not feel comfortable. It was really spooky. It made me think of the scene in the film *Marathon Man* where the evil dentist prepares to torture poor Dustin Hoffman. I knew that the Iranians wouldn't torture me, a western hostage, but I guessed that the gloves were there to frighten me.

Henry had a big stack of paper in front of him. He showed me the first form, which contained print-outs of photos from my phone which I'd taken in an art gallery in Tehran in 2019. 'Why did you photograph these paintings?'

'I liked the pictures,' I said.

'How were you able to visit the galleries?'

I said that an Iranian gallery owner, a friend, had brought Roland and me to visit several galleries one afternoon. Henry knew her name. 'She's not a good artist,' he declared.

'I haven't seen any of her work,' I replied. He wanted to know who was in her gallery when we met her. Once this was explained, I had to write my answer, in French, on his form, underneath the pictures in question.

Henry asked me why I had taken a picture of the logo of the Guardians of the Revolution. I told him I had taken it in the railway station in Rasht because I found the graphics interesting. I asked him if it was illegal to take a photo of the logo. He did not reply. Henry then asked about my travels. Had I been to Israel? I replied that I had been to Palestine and Jordan with Roland, visiting friends who worked for the World Bank. He kept saying 'Israel' and I kept answering 'Palestine'. More form-filling. Henry asked me the name of the person we had visited. I replied, 'David Craig'. David was director of the World Bank for Palestine at the time. He and his wife, Emilie, were very good friends. There was no point in lying because the Iranians had my computer. My response seemed to satisfy Henry for the time being. I was then brought back to my cell.

That afternoon, a guard took me from the cell, but instead of being left in the courtyard or the interrogation room, I was brought to the small visiting room, where I had to change out of my uniform. The guard explained in English that I was going to hospital for an examination, and they gave me my own clothes and boots. I had to put on a blindfold and handcuffs.

Outside, the guard put me into the back of a car. After a few minutes, the passenger in the front told me to remove the blindfold. We drove for about fifteen minutes through the city. I had no idea where I was. The streets and buildings looked unfamiliar. We then stopped in the forecourt of a hospital. In the reception area, many heads turned when they spotted a European in handcuffs. I was taken immediately into a side room for what turned out to be a blood test. They were probably checking if I was lying about my HIV status. Everything was very high-tech, with a screen on the wall into which the male nurse typed in my information. Nobody said anything. After a few minutes at the hospital, I was taken back to the interrogation centre.

Later that afternoon, I was subjected to more questioning. But first I asked George and Henry if the blood test was what they had called an 'examination'. George said that I would have to pay for an examination and he asked me to sign a document in Persian. I wrote in English that I was signing a document to pay for my blood test.

Now, Henry focused on David Craig, my friend at the World Bank. He claimed that David was a CIA agent. I said he was a retired banker from New Zealand. They had obviously been looking at my emails since they knew I had been advising Craig about a bridging loan for a new apartment. Henry suggested that this was strange for someone who ought to have the funds to buy an apartment. I asked him if he knew what a bridging loan was. He didn't, so I explained, but I am not sure he understood. He then asked me how I knew another friend, Lindy Foss-Quillet. He maintained that she, too, worked for the CIA. I explained that she was a new friend whom I had met a few weeks earlier at a friend's birthday party in Paris and we had planned to meet again on my return from Iran. Lindy, a UK–French dual national, is an artist with a studio near Paris.

I filled in more forms before being taken back to my cell. It was another hot night, and this time, when I called on the intercom for the fans to be turned off, a guard came immediately with pen and paper for me to write down my request. It worked. But the fans started whirring again about an hour later, and I couldn't get back to sleep. Having to sleep on the floor was aggravating a long-standing back problem, and lack of exercise meant that my knees were getting very stiff. I was now in constant pain. I was not sure if the sudden withdrawal from my medication was having an effect on me. I do not think I was depressed: I was too worried about what was going on to think of anything other than to survive as best I could, both physically and mentally.

The following day, the questions turned to the more problematic photos that I had taken on my current visit. Henry wanted to know why I had photographed the burnt-out mosque in Rasht. I explained that it was an unusual sight in a country as religious as Iran. I pointed out that on my phone he could find photos and videos of Notre Dame Cathedral burning because I'd been there on the day it went up in flames.

He turned to the picture of the police in Tabriz. Here I was less at ease. I pointed out that the photo was taken from the hotel's seventh floor at night. I said that seeing police using the hotel car park was a bit unusual. He continued asking about the video clip taken in Tabriz and I replied that it was not of a demonstration. In the clip, you can hear the demonstrators and see people marching in the distance but nothing close up.

Next came questions about the picture of the men I'd seen outside the juice bar in Orumiyeh. I indicated that they were not soldiers, as far as I could tell. They had no insignia on their clothes; they were just youths with helmets and truncheons. Then came a question about the photograph of the motor bikes with the blacked-out number plates. I explained that I was a motorcyclist. Henry asked me why I hadn't gone closer to get a better picture. I shrugged and told him he could find other motorbike pictures on my phone that had been taken in Iran and even a video I'd taken during a ride in Tehran. An Iranian friend had taken me on his scooter around the city. (I remember that there seemed to be no rules of the road, with us riding in the wrong lane against oncoming traffic and ignoring the traffic lights. Most of the other motorcyclists were not even wearing helmets. It had been a terrifying experience.)

After each question, if Henry seemed satisfied with my reply, he asked me to write my answer, in French, on the form. When I'd finished, he would come round the desk each time to take the forms to read. My handwriting is terrible, so he had difficulty deciphering what I had written. Occasionally he corrected my French grammar! His written French was almost as good as mine or maybe better. Because of his knowledge of the language, I wondered where and for how long he had studied French in France. At one stage, he came around to my left to read my replies and leant against me. I could feel the ridges of his corduroy trousers rubbing against me. I moved my chair to the right. Henry went back behind his desk.

It was an unnerving experience. What was he up to? Perhaps he was trying to provoke me.

Back in my cell, it was getting harder to spend the days alone. Apart from the questioning, I talked to nobody. I had nothing to read and found it very difficult to sleep, despite being exhausted. I need silence and a dark room to sleep well and this was most definitely not the case here. Every time I heard footsteps in the corridor, I wondered if they were to do with me. Who was in the other cells? Was Mike in this interrogation centre too? Astonishingly, I was beginning to almost enjoy the questioning sessions because they kept my mind busy.

For a few nights, a prisoner in the cell to my left was shouting in Persian. Some guards came and shouted back. Eventually I heard his door being opened and he was taken away. He must have been brought back at some point because the following night his bellowing began again.

At the next round of questioning, another man with a medical mask joined Henry and George. He had brought along my laptop. They wanted the passwords to my '1Password' account (a tool that manages all passwords) and to the mail server. I told them that I didn't know the passwords since they were all automatic and that if they had messed things up, it was their fault. The only person who could help them was my colleague David back at work! They weren't happy and scowled at me, but I just shrugged. I noticed that they had switched the language of the Mac to English. This meant that they were going to struggle with the French keyboard, but I said nothing. I did notice that the date was, in fact, 9 October, one day earlier than I had imagined. I was losing track of time.

On 10 October, the day I was due to fly home, George was alone in the interrogation room. He was snappily dressed, with an 'NY' baseball cap placed on the desk beside his leather briefcase. With a big smile, he said that he had good news for me: my sister Caroline now knew where I was. I had been worried all along that my family would think that I had had a car accident. I was so relieved that I broke down in tears. George then told me that I would shortly be transferred to the French authorities. I assumed he meant the embassy and I was suffused with happiness.

As I was led back to my cell, I felt as if I was walking on air. The guard gave me a comforting squeeze on my shoulder. Back in my cell, my mind kept busy trying to imagine what was going to happen next. How would I be taken to Tehran, almost 1,000 kilometres west of Mashhad? Would someone from the French embassy come to collect me? When would I be able to talk to Roland, my father and Caroline? Would I have to spend time in the French embassy before returning home?

♠ ♠ ♠

The next day, Henry questioned me on a new topic. 'We found two pieces of pottery in your rucksack,' he announced.

I remembered what had happened. On our way south to meet up with the main railway line between Tehran and Mashhad, Mike and I had stopped at a fortress that was undergoing restoration on the outskirts of the village of Esfarayen. We had to climb over a wall to get in. There was nobody around, but it appeared that repair work was underway, with lots of scaffolding and tools lying around. Outside the fort and beside the car, our hired driver was rooting around in the rubble beside a lean-to where mud bricks were drying out. He picked up some pieces of pottery and showed them to me.

One piece, about the size of my hand, had a blue motif and looked like a tile. The other was part of a jar, I thought. 'Take them,' the driver had said. 'They can be souvenirs.' I slipped them into my backpack.

I did not want to get the driver into trouble now, so I lied. 'I found them on the ground in an abandoned village.'

'Where exactly?'

I pretended to think about it before saying, 'I think it was along a dirt road near Raz. If you give me a map, I can probably point to where we were.' I kept it deliberately vague and they appeared to believe me.

After lunch, when I was taken back for questioning, Henry asked me with a smile if I liked the Iranian version of 'cassoulet' (a famous dish from the town of Castelnaudary, in south-western France). The Iranian version contains beans and pieces of meat but is nothing like the real thing.

'Oh, do you know the region?' I asked.

'I do,' he smiled, adding nothing further.

My supply of medication had now run out, but when I mentioned this, Henry and George simply said that they knew. I realised that my poor health might be the key to getting me out of prison. I thought that if the authorities saw that in addition to no longer having my medication, I was saying that I did not feel well, they might want to get me off their hands.

So that evening I called the intercom and said that I had a bad headache. The guard came with a tablet, which

I proceeded to hide in my mouth but then spat out in the toilet. Then I started to complain about my sore back. In truth, I was finding it more and more difficult to get up from the ground and needed to lean on the wall to help myself stand upright. I am a very active person and often try to do several things at the same time. Roland used to try and tell me to relax, but to no avail. I am often first up and last to bed, with two or three runs every week. My mind is usually full of things I need to do or get others to do.

Here, for the first time in my life, I could do absolutely nothing. My life was in the hands of my jailers.

I started to bang my head against the wall in frustration. Not too hard, but enough to be painful and maybe call their attention to the fact that I was not well mentally. There was no immediate reaction, but shortly afterwards, during an interview with George, I asked him when he was going to return my book. By now, I was desperate with boredom and needed some distraction. He said that he hadn't finished it yet. So I asked him if he could return one of my two guidebooks. Back in my cell a few hours later, the top hatch opened and there was my well-worn Lonely Planet guidebook to Iran. I proceeded to read the whole book from cover to cover, including the descriptions of all the country's hotels and restaurants. I knew that after this ordeal I would never come back to Iran, but reading the book helped to keep my mind occupied.

The Lonely Planet guidebook is probably the best for independent travellers to the country. However, Mike had explained that the latest edition was poorly updated because quite a few establishments no longer existed: the tourist industry in Iran is very fragile. It's true that practical information is very useful for first-time visitors, but some guidebooks do little to explain this very complex country, because they are written by outsiders.

♠ ♠ ♠

One day, I was taken out of the cell and led in a different direction. In the room I was brought to, I was told to sit. A man's voice said he was a doctor. Even with a blindfold on, I could just about see a white coat. He took my blood pressure and asked about my back. I said it was very sore from having to sleep on the hard floor. He told me he would give me something to relieve the pain, but nothing ever came.

I decided to be difficult. They were playing a game with me, between the visit to the clinic, this doctor's visit, not returning my books, making promises that I would be handed over to the French and not fulfilling them. That same evening, I refused my meal. This was clearly a problem. The guard shouted at me in Persian and I told him to bugger off – in English. I went and sat in a corner opposite the door. A while later the top hatch opened and a guard handed me a slip of paper and an ink pad. Using Google Translate, I worked out that they wanted me to write that I had refused my evening meal. So, to make life difficult for them, I wrote this in French in my worst handwriting and put my fingerprint on the form. They appeared satisfied. I did the same the next morning.

The daily questioning turned again to the political situation in France and to the Yellow Vest movement. I took a certain malicious pleasure in telling my questioners that they were out of touch with what was going on in France.

I said that perhaps they needed to change their embassy personnel.

Then they raised a new topic: my involvement in the Cox Bar in Paris. This is a well-known gay bar in central Paris, which I co-own. It has something of a militant reputation, largely because of me. Now, I tried to play down my role, saying that I was just a silent partner. However, early in 2022, I had been involved in organising an event to help the Ukrainian war effort with a French non-governmental organisation, raising funds to send medical supplies to the front. I knew the Iranian regime was pro-Russian, but nothing was said about that. However, George asserted that the LGBT lobby in Europe was powerful. I replied that he was correct in his assessment.

I finished the Lonely Planet book and asked for the return of my Bradt guide to Iran. This was more interesting to me because the first half covers the history and the present-day culture of Iran in great detail. The author, Maria Oleynik, is a friend of Mike's. I had talked to her once on the phone. She is Russian and speaks an amazing number of languages. She had studied at Trinity College Dublin and was now living in Shiraz, in the south of the country, a city I had visited twice. I read her book from cover to cover. Its publisher specialises in out-of-the-way destinations, such as Iran or Iraq, and it is completely different from the Lonely Planet guide because of its emphasis on culture and history.

My reading was interspersed with more questioning about awkward photos my interlocutors had found. This time it was a photograph taken of me, on my phone, at a beach outside Bouchehr on the Persian Gulf in February 2020. A friend of Mike's, a policeman, whom Roland suspected probably tortured prisoners part-time, had brought us there for a swim. I was the only one who went swimming. As I dried myself afterwards, I could see a manned anti-aircraft gun emplacement on the hill. In the photograph, it's in the background. We could also see the Bouchehr nuclear power plant from where we were.

'Tell me,' Henry said, 'who took this photo?'

'I can't remember,' I said. I was lying: it was actually Roland.

Henry got up from behind the desk, turned off the camera and came over to me. What's going on? I felt a little nervous. Is he going to hurt me, off camera, I asked myself. He leaned in close; I could feel his breath on my face. 'Maybe you might work for us? It might be good, no?'

The question took me aback. In exchange for what, I wondered – my freedom? 'I don't think so,' I said eventually. 'No.'

Henry didn't push the matter. I was brought back to my cell, but my mind was reeling from the question. What did they think they could get me to do back in Europe? Did they plan for me to befriend Iranian opposition organisations and send information back to them – in other words, did they want me to become a 'real' spy? The idea was ridiculous.

In the cell I tried to focus on positive things, forcing myself to think of Roland, Caroline, the house in Banyuls, my father in Dublin. I even started to imagine winning the lottery and that I would make it a surprise for Roland, turning up at his work in a taxi to take him to collect the cheque; and how we would spend the money. It made me smile. I decided that when I got out of this living night-mare, I would stop work, rather than waiting until I was the normal retirement age in France of sixty-seven. And my idea to buy a dog developed further: I would get another Labrador – a successor to my beloved Max, who had been my constant companion twenty years earlier. I would seize the day, rather than postponing things until some future date: I wanted to feel fully alive! Planning all this kept my mind busy. I tried not to think about the anxious concerns of my family back in France and Ireland.

♠ ♠ ♠

One morning, I was taken from my cell and guided to the small room with the one-way mirror. There I was given back my clothes. I had to put on the blindfold. I was handcuffed and shackles were attached to my feet. I was told that I was going to hospital again. I didn't argue: I was pleased to be leaving solitary confinement, even if just for a short while.

It was a long drive and I was allowed to remove the blindfold en route. The hospital was a modern building with soldiers at the entrance. The guards removed my shackles and brought me in through a side entrance. I was clearly expected: men in black suits were waiting for us. As usual, I got lots of stares from the public. Some people turned away, visibly unsettled to observe someone treated like this. A European would be a rare sight in Mashhad, I imagine, but one in this situation was probably more surprising. The hospital looked to be a private one and I wondered if this regime would take an Iranian political prisoner to a public hospital. I was not so sure.

We got into the lift, and I was taken to a big room and told to lie on a bed. There was a large television set on the wall, plenty of space, and even a phone beside the bed. Guards and other people were present. A doctor came in and explained, in English, that they were going to carry out some tests. A female nurse hooked me up to an ECG machine made by Siemens, which looked as if it had been purchased just the day before. The doctor examined me but said nothing. A blood sample was taken, then everyone left the room except for me and a guard.

After a long interval, everyone came back and I was handcuffed and taken downstairs to the basement and put in a large room with two beds and a separate toilet. This time I was handcuffed to the bed. A nurse came and hooked me up to a drip. There was no sign of the doctor, so I couldn't ask what they were giving me. I began to grow anxious, wondering what this was all about. Was my plan to focus on my 'bad' health working? Were the authorities afraid something might happen to me while I was in their hands and about how people would react in France and Ireland? But it was good to be out of solitary confinement. I was getting an insight into the Iranian healthcare system which, in this hospital, did not appear too bad. At least I was 'busy'.

Two guards were watching over me, a young man and an older man. There was a television set but the young man refused to give me the remote control or allow me to close the bathroom door when I went to use the toilet. Other than that, they didn't pay me much attention – the two of them were on their smartphones. Then the older man went out and came back in with bags of takeaway food, kebabs and rice, for them and me. It was the best food I'd had since my arrest, but it wasn't easy eating with one arm handcuffed to a bed! The older guard had Google

Translate on his phone, so I used it to ask him if he could give me something to help me sleep. He fetched a nurse and she added another drug to the drip.

One of the guards lay down on the other bed and the other slumped in a chair. The television was turned off and the lights turned down. It was the first time for I don't know how many days that I'd been able to go to sleep in a little darkness and silence. I fell asleep quickly but slept badly because I was handcuffed to the bed.

The next morning, after breakfast, the guards changed; this time there were three of them. I was allowed to have the TV remote control. Outside my room there appeared to be an office with a phone because I could hear people coming and going, making calls. A nurse came back in and changed the drip. After a while the blood started to flow back into the drip, as can sometimes happen. When I pointed this out to the guards, they panicked and two of them rushed out to get help. The nurse arrived and we both smiled because there was nothing to worry about, but it proved that the authorities were concerned about my health.

In the afternoon, there was another change of guards. This time there were two. One was very gentle and allowed me to eat without the handcuffs and also to close the door to the toilet. The rest of the time, I just lay on the bed and dozed, sometimes watching the television. This was my first encounter with Iranian state TV, a mishmash of religious programmes and news reports showing a lot of military activity, such as the test flights of rockets and drones.

Later that evening, one of the guards disappeared and the other went to sleep on the adjacent bed. I feverishly tried to think how I could get out and use the phone in the office next door to contact someone. I wondered where the sleeping guard kept the key to the handcuffs. I puzzled over what the number would be to get an outside line. Then I thought: would I be able to phone anyone outside Iran? What would the punishment be if I was caught? The thought of it made me quickly change my mind.

The next morning, there was another change of guard, this time to just the one. Perhaps I was becoming less dangerous! Perhaps they were about to take me to the French embassy in Tehran after all. This guard, with his baseball cap and hoodie, spent all the time on his smart-phone. He frequently left the room. I was really bored and uncomfortable because I could not move easily. I had not been able to wash since I'd arrived in the hospital and had not even been given a toothbrush. But I was focused on the prospect of imminent release that had taken hold in my imagination.

That afternoon, another guard arrived, and the nurse removed the drip. I still had no idea what had been in it and I didn't feel any different. I was taken out to an unmarked car and we drove off. No blindfold, just the handcuffs. The two guards seemed to think they were in a police movie. The driver put on the siren and drove at a furious speed on the dual carriageway, weaving in and out of the traffic. Both guards were laughing: a *Starsky and Hutch* movie, only in an old Peugeot. It brought to mind the world-beating numbers of Iranian deaths on the road; in one year as many as those in the 27 countries of the EU combined.

When the car left the dual carriageway, the guards asked me to shut my eyes because they had forgotten the blind-fold. So I pretended to keep them shut, but I was able to see that we were heading towards a cluster of buildings. We reached a huge pair of gates and, after the driver spoke to a guard, the car entered the compound and went along an unpaved road with a high boundary wall to my right and a windowless building to my left. The wall was topped with barbed wire – the kind that's embedded with razor-like blades. Armed guards patrolled the watch towers around the compound. We came through another gate and appeared to be on a street with shops. This, I realised, was a 'real' prison, not an interrogation centre. There were people going in and out, some in black uniforms and others with shopping bags crammed full of goodness knows what. I had visited prisons that were now museums, like Crumlin Road Prison in Belfast or Kilmainham Gaol in Dublin, but this was the real thing, just like in a film. This, I was to discover, was the main entrance to Mashhad Central Prison.

Chapter 6

Satan's Block

We drove into a yard and a metal gate closed behind us. I was taken from the car up some steps and into a reception area. My two guards handed over some paperwork to a uniformed guard at a computer screen. I was put into one of two holding rooms behind him; the other was for women prisoners. By this time, it was early evening and the sun had set. The place was very busy with what appeared to be petty criminals being released with sacks of their belongings. The men were scruffy, dirty and often had tattoos on their arms, teeth missing and the odd scar on their faces. The uniformed guard appeared to know some of them, so I figured it was not their first stay. He rubber-stamped their hands before they went out through the gate.

My turn came and I stood in front of the guard. The handcuffs were removed. He spoke English, asking me where I was from. I replied 'Ireland'. As a dual national, the rule is that I am French in France and Irish in Ireland. Elsewhere, my choice depends on the circumstances.

The guard asked me if I was from the North or the South of Ireland. In Iran, people generally know about the Troubles and the fact that the South, the Republic of

Ireland, is an independent state. He then asked me how I was. I told him that things were not great and that I had not been allowed to phone my family. The guard asked me for a telephone number, so I gave him Roland's and he promised that I would be allowed to call him the next day. I was then taken to be fingerprinted and photographed. I had to hold a card with a number on it in front of me. Next, a tall guard wearing big boots took me along a corridor which opened on one side to a large courtyard.

We came to a metal door manned by a guard, who took the paperwork and filled the details into a ledger, noting the time from a clock behind me. He opened the door and I entered a noisy room full of young guards in black uniforms and others with stripes on their shoulders. Here again, prisoners were arriving and leaving. I learned that this was where prisoners had their clothes checked. I sensed that I was the subject of some curiosity since many of those in the room had probably never met a European.

I was instructed to take off my clothes and boots but to keep on my underpants. The guards were wearing surgical masks and gloves. They had a metal trolley in front of them onto which I put my clothes. A guard asked me to open my mouth and proceeded to check if I was hiding anything in it. He didn't change gloves between prisoners, which frightened me because of Iran's terrifying Covid death rate. He then pulled the elastic of my underpants and gestured for me to turn around, taking a peek to see if I was concealing something in my underwear. Next, I had to show him the soles of my feet; then my shirt and socks were returned. My jeans, belt and boots were put in a cloth bag and I was handed a receipt for them. They gave me a pair of light blue trousers with white hems and a pair of white plastic flip-flops. Another uniformed guard took me out and down a long wide corridor, with well-kept potted plants along both walls. Everywhere was spotless. There were windows overlooking courtyards, but it was too dark to see anything outside. There were signs beside certain doors, in Persian and English. As we approached the end of the corridor, I could make out a barred entrance with prisoners noisily milling about behind it. Was this my destination? Just before the entrance gate, we stopped and the guard pressed a button beside a metal door to our right. We were buzzed in. This was block 6-1. I learned that because it housed prisoners facing the death sentence and serious political prisoners, it was known as Satan's block.

Inside, a few metres to the left, was the guards' office. They were all in civilian clothes. I could see a bank of computer screens with a live feed from the different cells and corridors. Paperwork was exchanged and a young prison worker (an inmate who worked for the prison authorities) took me through another metal door and into a corridor. I craned my neck to peer down a short turning to the right, a corridor which had two cell doors like the ones in the interrogation centres, with two hatches set into them. This, I was to learn, was where the prisoners are locked up the day before they are to be executed, after the call to morning prayers.

I didn't get to see much before I was whisked along the main corridor past more hatched doors, then three public phone boxes and a kitchen. At the very end of the corridor was an aviary. Birds in prison! It was hard to believe. Through a closed gate I could see out to the courtyard. We turned left into a stairwell, and I followed the prison worker upstairs. On the first floor, there were more plants along the wall, together with a folded red football table and a huge metal vent. I counted three doors on the left and three on the right of the corridor and wondered what was behind each of them. The prisoner worker opened the second door on the right. I walked in and the door slid shut behind me.

Part Two
The Prison Diary

Chapter 7

The Cell

17 October 2022. Since arriving in the cell, I have replayed my entrance over and over in my mind. After being moved from holding pen to holding pen, I wasn't aware at first that this final cell would become my home for an unknown period of time. After I settled in, I didn't want to forget that first alien moment of arrival. For me, my stay in prison was so real and vivid that I thought of it in the present tense.

The memory goes like this. In the cell, about eight metres by five metres, I count about ten faces looking up at me. A tall white man with long fair hair smiles and says hello. I cross over to him, holding out my hand. He introduces himself as Benjamin Brière. A Frenchman! What a relief: at last, somebody I can really talk to.

Benjamin tells me that that I have to take off my flip-flops and leave them on one of the three shelves to the left of the door.

Benjamin tells me this cell is for foreigners and Iranian political prisoners. It can hold up to 27 men if full! He has been in prison for over two and a half years. He was arrested in the region north of Mashhad near the border with Turkmenistan. He had a drone in his van and was accused of spying.

Benjamin then introduces me to our cellmates: three men from Bahrain, a man from Turkey and a young Pakistani, all of them imprisoned for drug trafficking. The cell also contains a young Iranian, Essan, who has serious mental problems and is a paedophile, whom I instinctively feel should have been placed in a mental hospital. Benjamin then introduces me to his closest friend, Taj, a political prisoner, along with three other Iranians also in the cell. They all smile and shake hands. I am offered tea and biscuits. I'm very hungry, not having eaten since leaving the hospital.

The cell has three large carpets on the floor on which we all sit. Three sides are lined with metal bunk beds three levels high. The remaining side, opposite the door, has windows set high up near the ceiling above a further set of bunk beds. At the other end are shelves, a television on the wall and a clock beside the ubiquitous photographs of Ayatollah Khomeini and the present Supreme Leader, Ayatollah Khamenei. Beside the door and the shelves for our flip-flops is a big old fridge held closed by a bungee cord. There's a bathroom area through a small opening in the wall, with two toilets, which are just holes in the ground, one shower, a sink with two sets of dripping taps in it for washing utensils, a separate wash-hand basin and a plastic mirror. Two big plastic bins sit in the shower area for washing clothes and a rope is strung across the top to dry them. (In Iranian prisons the prisoners do their own laundry.) Huge fans are set into the windows over the toilets. They make a noise like a 1990s washing machine on a spin cycle. The area also functions as a place to smoke and to store rubbish bins. On the wall are two bare wires where there should have been a light switch. To light a cigarette, the prisoner just touches the two wires together until they are red and then lights ups.

The oldest of the three Bahrainis, Abu Hassan – he's probably in his late fifties – tells me to take his lower bunk and that he'll sleep in the one above. He speaks a little English. I try to object, but he won't hear of it. He gives me a thermos flask for tea, and blankets are found, as well as a pillow. Someone uses the intercom to call down for a toothbrush and a towel for me. A few minutes later the hatch opens, and a prison worker passes through what we'd requested. Benjamin explains that if I want to take a shower, I should wait until after 10 o'clock, just after the night roll call, because that is when the water is hot. In the morning there is hot water until about 11 a.m. Thankfully, I am an early riser, so I manage to get to the shower while the water is still hot.

I am taken, with Benjamin as my translator into Persian, to the medical centre, for an electrocardiogram. The friendly nurse, whose name I catch as something like Josep, places the electrodes on my chest and starts the machine. He looks at the print-out and does another reading, a puzzled expression on his face. 'Do you have a heart problem?'

'Yes, and I need medical treatment for it,' I say. He scribbles something on a piece of paper and I am brought to another room, where a doctor writes out a prescription. 'Everything is fine,' he beams.

'Why are you writing out a prescription with five different things on it, if "everything is fine"?' I ask. He does not reply.

'I don't trust the prison authorities and I don't trust you,' I say. 'I won't take your medication.' He just shrugs and Benjamin and I return to the cell.

The evening prison meal is wheeled into our block through the main door on a trolley with two huge pots and fresh bread on it. The job now is for the prison workers to divide the food into smaller pots according to the number of prisoners in each cell. It's a very ad hoc affair and pieces of bread fall on the floor. Some of the food is put in individual plastic containers: I learn that this is for certain cells where the men are facing execution the next morning.

Prison workers are prisoners themselves. These prisoners do the day-to-day work on the blocks, such as cleaning, delivering food and running errands for the guards. They also take other prisoners to the medical wing, to the gym or the library. Each block has a prison-worker manager, also a prisoner, who organises the team. Some of these workers can move freely around the prison. The prison workers in the medical wing all wear a pale blue shirt with a Mao collar. The prison workers who work in the kitchen are similarly easy to recognise because they all wear a bright orange uniform.

Just before 10 p.m., a voice comes over the loudspeaker. Benjamin explains that this is the last of the three daily roll calls. We all have to kneel in rows on the floor. The door opens and a civilian guard and a prison worker enter and count us. The guard has a smile for me when he asks my name and I reply, 'Bernard Phelan. Father, Vincent'. As soon as he leaves, I head for the shower. The door and wall are at shoulder height, and I use a bit of cardboard to wedge the door shut. It's my first proper shower since my arrest. Lots of hot water, and Benjamin has kindly given me some shampoo and soap.

Benjamin shows me his collection of books. It's great to be able to speak in French, which nobody else in the cell can understand. Benjamin got the books from his family and friends through the French embassy in Tehran. At the beginning of Benjamin's imprisonment, the embassy printed off copies of books by Jules Verne for him. I tend only to read books in English, but he recommends a detective novel in French, *L'Affaire Alaska Sanders* by a Swiss author, Joël Dicker. I am so happy to finally have something I'll probably enjoy, apart from my guidebooks to Iran.

The sound of the television in the cell is turned down to a whisper. I go to bed and start to devour Dicker's novel. The lights are never turned off, so we are allowed to put curtains across part of our bunks to block out the light. There is a CCTV camera over the fridge where the guards can see everyone. There is also one in the toilet area. Around 11 p.m. the guards remotely turn off all the televisions in the block. However, the lights still blast away all night, making sleep near-impossible.

Chapter 8

Life in Prison

24 October 2022. My promised phone call to Roland didn't materialise. Neither was it permitted the next day, or the next. I realised I might be waiting a while. Now, a week after my arrival and my first, alien, day, I am still waiting.

I am now well acquainted with the morning routine. The first call to prayer, at 4 a.m., wakes me up and I see my religious cellmates going to the bathroom to wash, to take out their prayer mats and turn them towards Mecca, which is in the direction of my bunk. So, for example, Abu Hassan, who has the bunk above me, prays just a few centimetres from me. There's not much noise, but one of the younger men tends to cry a lot, which I find disturbing. I recognise the word 'Allah' as he pleads in prayer with tears rolling down his cheeks.

A hot-water urn and food for breakfast are delivered by a prison worker. At about 8 a.m. there is the first roll call, so everyone has to get up. Ibrahim, one of the Bahrainis, stays in bed until the last moment before tumbling to the floor. After the prisoner count, most people go back to bed. Abu Hassan has the job of sharing out whatever we have got for breakfast. This can be a feta-like cheese that has to be cut up for each prisoner, often accompanied by dates. On other days we might get small tubs of carrot jam, an Iranian speciality, or bars of halva, a Middle Eastern delicacy made from almonds; it's very sweet. Bread, delivered the evening before, is in a bin beside the water urn. There is also a plastic tub of loose tea leaves and another containing rice.

I eat my breakfast standing up, using the bunk above Benjamin's as a table. After breakfast, it's off to the bathroom for a hot shower. The toothbrush the prison gave me broke in two on the first morning I used it.

In the cell there's a rota for cleaning, which is stuck up beside the prayer schedule. Normally, a different prisoner cleans the cell every day. This is usually done when the rest of us are in the yard. It involves taking up the long thin cushions beside each bunk and sweeping the room. The rubbish is taken down to the yard. The bathroom and toilet area are cleaned in the evening when everyone has washed their pots and dishes after dinner. The prison supplies the cleaning products. Because Reswan, the Pakistani, has no way of getting money, most of us pay him the equivalent of less than one euro to do our turn on the rota. The 'accounting' is managed by the prison worker who runs the shop. Reswan also earns money by doing laundry, except underpants, for fellow prisoners, including those from other cells in our block.

We are allowed to leave the cell to walk in the courtyard twice a day for 45 minutes. The times at which we are let out change about every fifteen days, so all the cells in our block get a fair turn. Officially, there should never be any mixing of prisoners. However, prisoners are regularly being moved around for various purposes, so you do meet some of the long-term prisoners. On top of which, news travels extremely fast, so everyone knows there's an Irishman in the cell with Benjamin.

This courtyard break is also the time when we can make phone calls (within Iran only) and use the kitchen. There is a longer kitchen time in the evening of about an hour and a half when the gate to the courtyard is shut and sealed by a guard. I have no idea why because there is no way anyone could escape from the courtyard.

Benjamin explains that I have to apply for a phone card to use the phone, which means listing up to five Iranian phone numbers I wish to call. I also have to ask for a prison debit card to be able to buy things in the block's shop. Benjamin lends me his card to call the French embassy in Tehran. He warns me that a recorded message plays about every two minutes informing the receiver of the call that it is from a prisoner.

I get through to the consul, Christian Furceri, and he's expecting my call. It's quite emotional because he has news from my family. He is also able to give me the mobile number of the Irish chargé d'affaires, Justin Ryan, who is based in the German embassy in Tehran. The Irish have reduced their presence in the country and the ambassador to Iran is presently based in Ankara. I am able to dictate messages immediately to everyone back in Europe, a task that makes me break down in tears. I ask Furceri if he knows anything about my medication. He explains that Roland has delivered a consignment to the ministry in Paris and that it will be in the *valise diplomatique* (diplomatic pouch) which arrives in Tehran every Sunday. The medication will be brought to the Iranian Ministry of Justice for onward shipment to Mashhad. The consul thinks it will take another week for it to reach me. He explains that a consular visit has been requested for me, but it's up to the Iranian authorities to approve it.

I cannot call Justin Ryan because he is not on Benjamin's card, but I can now add his number to my phone-card request, as well as the mobile number of Benjamin's lawyer, Ms Halami.

By the time I finish my call, there are other prisoners waiting to use the phone, so there's not much time for a stroll in the courtyard.

The courtyard is about 25 metres long and ten metres wide. The walls are about seven metres high. At one end there is a tiled flowerbed with plants, including two banana trees. At the other end are the refuse bins, which are taken away each day. Leftover rice is put on the ground to feed the sparrows and pigeons and the ground around the bins is littered with dead cockroaches. Otherwise, every surface in the prison is extremely clean. In Iran, there is a strong emphasis on cleanliness, both personal and in any public spaces. A stone bench is situated just to the right of the gate and there's a bench along the opposite wall. The outdoor gym equipment is never used by the prisoners. It appears that nobody is interested in keeping fit. Perhaps the prison workers use the equipment when we are locked in our cells, or maybe the other gym, which Benjamin and I are not allowed to go to, is better.

In front of one of the barred windows on a corridor in block five, there's a small plastic crate tied to the window ledge. Benjamin explains that the prisoners use it to try to catch pigeons. I have never seen pigeons approaching this crate, I assume because they don't want to become someone's dinner.

81

Benjamin and I sit on the stone bench, soaking up the late autumn sun and chatting. Most of our cellmates are walking in pairs up and down the yard. Reswan and Taj tend to walk together. Karim and Morthasa speed-walk in step with each other. The others are with prison workers, either strolling around or sitting on the bench smoking and chatting. Because of the high walls that surround us, it feels a bit like walking along the bottom of a deep, empty swimming pool. There is a camera at the far end of the courtyard: nobody is certain if it can pick up sound, so we tend to talk at the opposite end of the yard.

Benjamin tells me that the 'criminal' prisoners rarely discuss their crimes, so it's a matter of piecing together snippets of information gleaned from them and others. I know Mashhad is an important platform for drug trafficking owing to its proximity to Afghanistan, which is about 150 km to the east, and to an international airport with direct flights to Dubai, Abu Dhabi and Ankara, among other cities.

First, he tells me about the three Bahrainis, who are in prison for drug-trafficking offences. The two younger ones are cousins and they sleep on the lower bunks opposite us. Abdullah, 'the youngest of the three', used to be a policeman in Bahrain dealing with traffic offences. His cousin, Ibrahim, 'the sleepiest of the three', is a drug pro. Apparently, he knows everything there is to know about drugs, their chemical composition and the effects they have on those who use them. He has money and pays for everything for the other two. He gets methadone daily from a nurse from the medical centre. Abu Hassan, nicknamed 'the oldest of the three', has been in jail before, as have the others, but not in Iran. He is a very religious Muslim.

These three have already been guests of similar establishments for drug trafficking in Kuwait, Saudi Arabia and the United Arab Emirates.

The Turkish man, Hassan, speaks good English, and is nicknamed Yellow Vest, like the French protesters, because he often wears a yellow shirt. He was a truck driver and was caught with a huge load of heroin. He barely escaped the death penalty, being sentenced instead to over twenty years of imprisonment. He has been in Mashhad prison for about seven years. I'm told he is a nasty piece of work, a real hypocrite who loves to stir up trouble.

Next is Reswan, from Pakistan. He's in his early twenties, from a peasant background, and is also very religious. He apparently got caught at Mashhad airport transporting drugs for someone back in Pakistan. He is married with a very young daughter and claims that he did not know that he was transporting drugs. His sentence has not been handed out, but it's understood by all that he isn't going home anytime soon. He has a bunk at the end of the room near Yellow Vest.

Essan is the young, mentally ill Iranian I met on my first day, who is inside for molesting a child. He is nineteen, and he lived in Mashhad with his parents before coming to prison. He does not speak much. Because of his intellectual difficulties, the other prisoners look after him, giving him food and clothes. He has a second-level bunk just beside the cell door.

Taj, one of the political prisoners, is 47 years old and has already spent seven years in prison. He is from Bojnurd, a town I passed through with Mike on our way to Mashhad, where he ran an import–export business. He imported German medical equipment and exported liquid petroleum gas to Pakistan. A religious Sunni Muslim who spent ten years in a madrasa (a school of Islamic instruction) in Pakistan, Taj is married and his wife tries to visit him regularly. He has been condemned to death, along with five others. When he will die, he doesn't know. He could be in prison for years first – this is part of the punishment for political activities in Iran. He speaks a little English as well as Urdu, so he helps Reswan a lot. Taj has a lower bunk on our side of the cell. The bunk above his bed contains all the belongings he has accumulated over seven years.

Next to be profiled is Karim, also in his twenties, a good-looking man who is tall and well built. He is from Torbat, a town about 90 km to the south of Mashhad, where he worked as a mason. Karim is divorced with a young daughter. He had been out on parole (a common practice in Iran) and was brought back for two months but is still being held six months later. His bunk is behind mine but on the next level up.

Morthasa, a young shepherd, is also from Torbat. A small, strapping man in his early twenties, he is always laughing and trying to joke, but not afraid to speak his mind. He seems to be a good friend of Karim, and so far, he's been very friendly to me too. He has the bunk below Karim's.

Then there's The Dog, the boss of the cell. Benjamin doesn't know his real name – he is just known as The Dog. He is hated by everybody. He has the bunk at the end of the room, but apparently he tends to move to a different bunk from time to time. His belongings seem to be spread across three empty bunks.

The loudspeaker in the yard comes on to tell us that it's the end of our period out there. A prison worker rounds us up and locks us into our cell. There, Benjamin starts to fill me in on his case and his years in prison. He tells me that he had been on a road trip from France in a van, having taken leave from his work in the Gulf. Benjamin had worked most of his life abroad in Dubai and Tokyo. In Tokyo, he met his last girlfriend, the daughter of the Algerian ambassador to Japan. In Dubai, he organised concerts and sporting events. He had taken leave of absence for his road trip to northern Iran and was due back in Dubai as part of the team helping to manage the 2023 World Cup in Qatar. He had spent a long time in Iran, staying here during the last Covid lockdown.

When he was arrested, he was handled roughly by the security people. He was initially imprisoned in a much smaller prison in a city north of Mashhad. That's where he'd picked up most of his pretty fluent Persian because almost nobody there spoke English and nobody at all spoke French. After a few months, he was moved to Mashhad. That was, I think, when he started to have some contact with the French embassy in Tehran. The previous ambassador never visited him in prison.

Benjamin had had a stormy relationship with the embassy before I arrived. He had asked to have no more consular visits from Christian Furceri. Furceri was married to an Italian who lived in Rome with their daughters. According to Benjamin, the man appeared to know little about Iran. I think he never moved from Tehran except for consular visits to Mashhad and Shiraz, where there was another French prisoner, Olivier (his last name was never made public). Furceri's reports back to Benjamin's family consisted of three words; 'Benjamin is fine!' Benjamin says that he does not want to be in debt to the French authorities by asking them to send him things, such as clothes or books. Everything he has was sent from France by his family and friends. In spite of this, he appears to have settled into a good routine, thanks to his leather workshop. He learned to work with leather in the previous prison and now knows lots of the people working in the block. Because of his workshop, he's been able to meet many other political prisoners in our block.

Benjamin finds me a metal plate and a spoon to use as cutlery. There are no knives or forks. He explains that when the block's shop opens this evening, I can use his debit card to buy various bits and pieces. Lunch arrives, usually in two big pots, along with fresh bread. Unfortunately, the food is never very hot, so if our court-yard break is around lunchtime, I take the food down to the kitchen and heat it up. So far, it's usually been rice and an indescribable stew, which is sometimes almost black or dark green. At other times there are bits of chicken floating in it with lentils, or occasionally there's just one pot with rice and tinned tuna in it, which is accompanied by tubs of yogurt.

After lunch I try to doze, like most of my cellmates, but it's not easy with the television on and the fans whining, so I end up reading instead.

At around 4 p.m., the second roll call takes place. After that, things get busy in the cell, with most of us starting to prepare food for our evening meal. Some prisoners, like the three Bahrainis, prepare their meals together. It's a very sociable occasion because you often have to borrow a pot or another kitchen utensil from a cellmate. Because there are no knives, the tops of cans are used to chop the food. Abu Hassan has a strip of fine sandpaper (I have no idea where he got it) to make these pieces of tin razor sharp. Everyone cuts himself at some stage. There is also a knife in the cell which one of the prisoners has made and kept hidden and we all use it discreetly. There is even a vegetable peeler, which, for some weird reason, we nickname Macron.

Chapter 9

A Shared Meal

One day, Taj invites Benjamin and me to share his dinner, so we help with the peeling and chopping. As the time approaches for us to be allowed down for the one and a half-hour evening break, people gather near the cell door with their pots, food, cooking oil and spices, ready to dash downstairs to the kitchen and secure a gas ring.

Everything has to be arranged so we finish in time to be locked up for the night. Taj is so well organised; he even has a plastic tablecloth, which he spreads on the ground, offering us tissues to use as napkins. He has made a delicious meal with aubergines, onions, tomatoes and lots of garlic. He puts the food in the middle and we all sit around with our own plates, spoons and cups. We eat in silence and afterwards he offers us dates that he has bought in the shop. Taj tends to buy big stocks of things from the shop because he knows the item in question may not be available again for some time. I saw him once come out of the shop with at least ten boxes of dates, and another time with lots of boxes of tissues.

Essan, the prisoner with mental health issues, is always first to stand in front of the door at break-times. He's sometimes there for an hour before we are allowed out.

He gets very confused when the time changes – about once every fifteen days – for us to go down. The other prisoners try to explain that's it's not time yet. Essan gets so impatient, he calls down to the guards' office. He usually gets told off.

When we are allowed out, I go with Benjamin to the shop, which is right next door to our cell. It used to be a small prison cell. There, I am introduced to the shopkeeper, a prison worker. There are two fridge freezers in the cell and shelves of food and toiletries, along with some clothes, underwear and shirts. I buy two short-sleeved shirts and two pairs of underpants; one is covered with a picture of Mickey Mouse! I order an extra pair of trousers, since it's unlikely that I'll get my jeans back. We also buy a new toothbrush, toothpaste, shampoo, disposable razors, shaving cream, sweets, biscuits, tins of tuna and maize, cooking oil, eggs, pasta, a box of dates, a copybook and pens. By European standards the items are all very cheap, so when I get my own debit card, I often buy sweets or biscuits to give to my cellmates. There's even Coca-Cola and Sprite, which is very popular with the prisoners. These drinks are manufactured under licence in Iran despite all the US sanctions. Benjamin stocks up on cigarettes: a carton costs three euro.

Some of the fresh food looks dubious. There are tomatoes in a crate, not in great condition, but there's no choice. There's butter, but it's rancid. The freezer contains frozen chicken, but Benjamin tells me that you cannot be sure how it was transported to the prison. The frozen chicken could have thawed out and been frozen again, and the last thing I want is food poisoning. Benjamin hands over his debit card and calls out the PIN code. (This is normal in Iran.) We carry our supplies back to the cell before heading downstairs to help Taj in the kitchen.

The kitchen usually has prison workers in it, so there's a certain competition for one of the six gas rings. The one beside the door is not popular because of the incoming draught. The kitchen has a big water boiler at the far end beside the windows. There is no glass in these windows because, I think, the authorities want the kitchen well ventilated. There is a large sink and a table. Usually one ring is always alight and because there are no matches and lighters are not allowed in the prison, pieces of spaghetti have been placed in a cup to light the other rings. Each person has a small towel for handling the hot pots and pans. People keep coming and going, making phone calls or smoking beside the locked gate into the courtyard, the only area except for the shop that has no CCTV cameras.

Benjamin shows me his leather workshop, which is near the kitchen, in an old cell opposite that of the prison workers. There are about ten workers in this cell. From what you can see from the cell's open door, it looks a lot more comfortable than ours. In Benjamin's workshop he has a small table for one person to work at and shelves around the wall. A CCTV camera sits on the wall in the corner. It's a popular spot for prisoners to chat. Because he can work here outside normal hours, he has been able to meet most of the prisoners in the block. News and information circulate this way, too. Prisoners can give Benjamin a message to be passed on when another group are on their break, because the prisoners from one cell are never allowed to mix with those from other cells.

Benjamin has a great variety of tools, which he has accumulated over time. He is a meticulous worker who hates disorder, so when the place is left in a mess by the prison workers, he's not happy. He has a stock of leather, which he keeps in our cell over his bed. Benjamin has been able to buy templates from outside the prison, like the rest of his tools, by paying a guard to do this for him. So when, for example, he wants to make a bag, he traces the different parts he needs, then cuts out the pieces that have to have holes punched in them. The next part, the sewing, can be done in the cell.

Outside the leather workshop is a small letter box. Guess what it's for? Suggestions from prisoners for the prison authorities! I never saw it used.

We use this dinner break to make phone calls, if the times correspond to office hours in Tehran, but the prison workers tend to monopolise one or two phones, so this is difficult. They have free movement all day in the block, even after everyone is locked up for the night. (Apparently, there is a rule that the workers must leave two phones for the prisoners' use. I have discovered that, like many rules, this one is not enforced.) The worst offender is the prisoner manager, who is in charge of controlling all the prison workers in our block. He also has the concession for the shop next door to our cell. He gets a percentage of the turnover from the shop, and because our block contains mostly political prisoners, the shop does quite well. Some prisoners are doctors or ex-politicians, so they have family and friends who can send them money without any problem.

Most of the prisoners take some of the prison food and keep it in the fridge. They will mix it later with food they themselves have cooked. After the evening meal, some of the prisoners start playing backgammon or just chat. At 7 p.m., we have news on the TV, which we nickname 'the hour of lies'. In prison we see only the state channels: there are many and they include an English-speaking station called Press TV. The evening news tends to be focused on the price of chicken, engine oil, bread and eggs. With inflation going up all the time in Iran, the news reporter goes into shops to ask people about the current prices of various things. There are also usually spokesmen from the Ministry of Foreign Affairs and/or the Ministry of Justice giving out about something the West has done. The news also runs lots of pictures of the latest Iranian missiles and drones. At the end of the bulletin, some poor family who have lost a loved one recently, or in the Iran–Iraq war nearly forty years ago, is interviewed. There's little international news and no weather forecast. The advertising is usually for three or four different companies, all of which, I heard, were owned by the Guardians of the Revolution or the clergy. The Iranian population do not watch this rubbish: they all tune into satellite channels beamed from the Gulf states.

Lying in my bed, I have a good view of the television. Benjamin and Taj explain what's going on. After the news, there's often a film, usually some US thriller, or an Iranian historical series. The prisoners at the far end of the cell bring their pillows and blankets closer to the television. There's also a business going in bootlegged DVDs, and one of the prisoners has bought in a DVD player. If you have enough money, you can buy certain things like a DVD player, a television, a fridge, pots and pans. The DVDs are usually of violent American films, dubbed into Persian. Any scenes with women are cut. The original language version isn't available, as that would mean more work for the censors, according to Taj!

A little later, the hatch opens and medication is distributed. A prison worker and a male nurse have small tubs with the prisoners' names on them. The medication, tablets and/or powder is poured into the prisoner's hand. Each prisoner must then swallow his dose in front of the nurse and prison worker.

The final roll call of the day takes place at 10 p.m. It's funny to see the prison guard in his stockinged feet looking serious with his clipboard.

Earlier, in the kitchen, I'd gone to the gate in the yard to look at the moon through the bars. It was strange to think that thousands of miles away, my family and friends might be looking at it too.

Chapter 10

A Visit from George

One morning the door slides open and I am called outside. Benjamin offers to accompany me but the prison worker refuses. I am not told where I am going. Benjamin asks the man what he wants me for, but he gets no reply. The prison worker silently accompanies me downstairs.

It has taken me some time to decode the ranking system of the guards and staff and their different uniforms. Apart from the prison workers, the next broad group are civilian employees, who dress in street clothes. They work on the administrative side of the prison, for example watching the CCTV cameras, or working in the medical wing. The most senior group are non-civilian employees. The (usually armed) prison officers wear a uniform with stripes on their shoulders according to their rank. Then there are the men doing their military service, who are generally quite young, in their early twenties, and only seem to carry a gun when on the minibuses taking prisoners to court, or to another external location. Finally, there are fully fledged army men, dressed in the desert khaki uniform. Sometimes they even wear flak jackets. They are posted in places like the entrance, where clothes are checked, and they are used to escort individual prisoners to the control room when leaving the prison or to the meeting room for consular visits.

In one corridor at the bottom of the stairs on my block are other prisoners whom I have never seen before. There's an old man, very erect, with an incredibly wrinkled face. He says hello in English and shakes my hand. The prison worker tells him off and we continue to the door beside the prison guards' office. I am instructed to wait. To my left is a curtain, which is drawn. I later discover that there's a window behind the curtain that looks into one of the two cells for condemned prisoners.

Another prison worker comes out of the prison security department, which I shall visit frequently over the coming months. We pass through an office with two desks and then into a short corridor before entering another office. To my surprise, George is there, along with two men.

'Hello,' I say. 'How about returning my book to me?' He borrowed *The Forging of a Rebel* by Arturo Barea when we first met and he still has it. He smiles and says he has not finished it yet.

'I'm here to talk about the pottery, do you remember?'

Of course I remembered.

'The two pieces in your bag are very old, did you know that?'

'No.'

'Well, they are. Nine hundred years old.' He waits for my reaction. When I offer him nothing, he says, 'I need you to sign a statement. You must say that you took them.'

'I won't,' I replied. 'No statement.'

He thinks for a bit, then says, 'Will you record a statement then?' Another man takes out a video camera. 'You just say that you shouldn't have taken the pieces of pottery.'

'No,' I insist. 'I will not say that I took them. But,' I add, 'I will say that it was a mistake to have taken them away.'

He shrugs and agrees. So, facing the camera, I make the statement. When I've finished, George leans back in his chair, smiling, and says, 'I hope you like being in the same cell as your French friend.'

'I do,' I agree. 'But why did you tell me that I'd be transferred to the French embassy soon?'

'Things have changed' is all he says. What these 'things' are, he doesn't say. I know that there is no point in asking, because my question will be greeted with a shrug.

The prison worker, waiting outside, is called in to take me back to my cell. I wash my clothes for the first time because it's early morning and there is hot water. I find some detergent and fill one of the plastic bins in the shower cubicle with hot water. I strip down to my underpants, get into the bin of hot water and scrub the clothes as best I can. After rinsing everything, I hang the clothes on the lines in the cubicle. The atmosphere is very dry, so the clothes dry quickly.

Back in the cell and sitting on the floor, I write up messages to be dictated later to the consul in Tehran. Suddenly Abu Hassan comes from the bathroom, very agitated. It turns out that I should not have hung my underpants up there to dry! It's explained to me that there's a washing line on the wall beside my bunk for hanging my underpants. One learns something new every day.

I am concerned that I shall soon have gone a whole month without medication. For the moment, there are no visible side-effects from the sudden withdrawal of medicine, but I know that some of the tablets I usually take should not be stopped abruptly.

Benjamin is allowed to go to his leather workshop down-stairs outside our cell's normal courtyard hours. Every day, he calls on the intercom and a prison worker comes and collects him. I am rather jealous of his extra freedom.

After lunch, the hatch opens and my phone card is handed in at last. This means that I can call Justin Ryan, the Irish chargé d'affaires, and dictate a message to my father. When it's our turn to go out, Benjamin uses his debit card to put money on my phone card. I get through to Justin. I am so happy to hear an Irish accent that I start to cry. Justin is really patient, explaining that the Irish Department of Foreign Affairs is doing everything possible to get me out.

He also says that he has requested a consular visit and is waiting for a reply from the Iranian authorities. He has regular meetings with his counterparts at the French embassy. Justin asks me if there's anything I want: he can post things to the prison. I ask for books in English, the *Irish Times* Simplex crosswords, notepads, pencils and a rubber, socks, jumpers, a woollen hat and underpants. He says that he will let me know when it's all posted. He is in Tehran with his wife and children, who are attending the international German school. He tells me that he is also responsible for Irish prisoners in the United Arab Emirates. I imagine he thought that he was in for a relatively quiet posting until I turned up!

I dictate the letter to my father. Justin will arrange for the Department of Foreign Affairs in Dublin to print it out and post it, so my father should be reading it in a few days.

Chapter 11

Doctor Honey

One morning shortly after breakfast, a prison worker comes and asks me to follow him. Downstairs, beside the guards' office, there is a clothes rail with gold-coloured waistcoats on it, each with a number on the back. I am invited to put on one of these and the guard buzzes the door out of our block. We step into a big corridor, which is busy with people coming to work and groups of other prisoners wearing different-coloured waistcoats. I work out that the red ones are for the prisoners in block 5 and white ones are for young prisoners. With the prison worker, Hussein, who is in for rape, I cross the corridor and enter the medical centre. A prison worker at a desk is told who I am. We pass a room with a proper barber's chair and I notice a prison worker cutting a prisoner's hair. Then we pass a shop, which is a little bigger than the one in block 6-1, before making our way down a corridor to a desk, where Hussein gives the guards my name.

In the corridor, we pass rows of seated prisoners waiting outside the doors to various departments. Over each door is a sign in Persian and English: DENTIST, X-RAY, PHARMACY and so on. There's even a sign with the word 'Buttery'! The pharmacy has a hatch where prison workers hand in slips to obtain the medication for prisoners in the various blocks. Some prisoners wave at me or say 'hello' in English. Most, I assume, have never seen a 'real' European and I get noticed immediately. We walk into a small office, with a sign above the door, DOCTOR. Inside, three desks have been squeezed together. There are other prisoners already there but they are all ushered back out to the corridor by prison workers wearing smart pale blue shirts.

One of the doctors waves me into a chair, shakes my hand and introduces himself in English. I was to nickname him Dr Honey because his name sounded something like that. He takes my blood pressure and pulse. He apparently knows some of my medical history; in particular that I have a heart condition and HIV. I explain that I am now approaching one month without medication for these conditions, and that I also take a daily treatment to reduce the risk of a stroke, as well as an antidepressant. He explains that he can source Iranian medication for me. I say that I trusted nobody in the prison and that I would wait until my medication arrived from France. He warns me that I am taking a big risk. I agree, but since it's the Iranian authorities who are responsible for me being incarcerated, they and the prison authorities will get the blame if anything happens to me. He pleads with me to at least take something for my blood pressure. I reply that if his medication brings down my blood pressure, the prison can say that I am in good health, which would neither be accurate nor helpful to my cause.

I am then taken to another room where, once more, the other prisoners are ushered out. I'm to have a blood test. A doctor asks me to roll up my sleeve. He does not wash his hands or clean my skin, nor does he use a tourniquet. He just grabs my upper arm, jabs in the needle, takes the sample and gives me a small piece of cotton wool to soak up the blood.

After that, it's back to the cell for me.

On television we see that there's been a riot in Evin prison in Tehran, where most foreign hostages are kept. There's been a fire, which has killed four prisoners, and a lot of others have been injured. The idea of a fire in prison haunts me. How would you escape between the metal door and the barred windows? There are no fire extinguishers in the block. In fact, I never see any in the prison.

Chapter 12

My First Call Home

30 October 2022. More hard-boiled eggs for lunch. They get pretty boring with just salt, but I can't face not eating them. The salt isn't great for my blood pressure, especially now that I'm off medication. I've started writing the date on the eggs, so I'll know when to eat them. I gather from Benjamin that we get more food in our block than certain other blocks do. He told me that he persuaded the block manager to distribute the leftover food to other blocks.

Eating on the floor is a real pain. My back wasn't in great shape before I was imprisoned, and between the bed with its rigid base and no mattress and the hard floor, the pain is getting worse. It's a throbbing pain along the base of my spine which never disappears. Getting out of bed or standing up off the floor is becoming increasingly painful.

After lunch, I try to snooze, but with the television on it's impossible to sleep. Yellow Vest puts on the English-speaking state channel Press TV, which churns out anti-Western propaganda under the slogan 'The Voice of the Voiceless'. I'm feeling really run down. The presenter's American accent and the rubbish he is transmitting are really hard to take. I wonder how Europeans can work for a television station like this. Their correspondent in

Brussels has an Irish accent. I think if I ever meet him, I will tell him a few home truths. Benjamin and I talked about throwing the remote control down the toilet. He told me how he had once taken the batteries out of the handset and thrown them out of one of the few barred windows that we can open.

The Press TV channel loves to show anything negative going on in the West, be it a strike, a forest fire, an accident, or people trying to cross the English Channel. It's so depressing. I cannot even escape through sleep until I get my sleeping tablets each night. Sleep is what I yearn for because when I'm asleep, my brain shuts out anything bad. I never have nightmares in prison and I always wake up in good form, fully rested. I have no idea what the nurse from the medical centre gives me each evening but it works.

When prisoners have questions or requests for the prison authorities, we have to complete a form that we buy in the shop. We have to indicate to whom we are writing within the prison system, and the subject matter. For this part we get help from Taj or Karim and the rest is written in English, dated (in the Persian calendar, 2022 is the year 1401)[1], signed and fingerprinted with the inkpad. My first form went in a couple of days ago, a request to phone my family.

---

[1] Coming from its pre-Islamic past, this solar calendar divides the year into 12 months, with the New Year occurring in spring at the time of the equinox (Nowruz festival). The division of months is very different from the Western calendar: the first six months have 31 days, the next five months have 30 days, the last month 30 days or 31 for leap years. Curiously, the Islamic Revolution left this calendar in place, without imposing the Muslim calendar. Source: *Hachette Guide Bleu Usage Et Coutumes d'Iran*, p. 55.

Today, on my first-ever permitted call to anywhere outside Iran, I get through to Roland. I have a list of things to ask him but, instead, we just laugh with joy at being able to talk to each other and I forget the list. During the call, I am filmed by a guard. I have been told to speak in English and not to talk about my condition or about that of other prisoners. However, Roland says he will speak only in French which, knowing Roland, does not surprise me. We talk about anything and everything, about the house in Banyuls and all the work that he and our friends are doing on it. After about ten or fifteen minutes, the guard gestures to me that my time is up. I go back to my cell with a big smile on my face.

The following morning I am brought to security, along with Benjamin as a translator. There's a promising-looking delivery from Irish diplomat Justin Ryan. I open it eagerly. Before I can take away the books in the parcel, I'm required to list the book titles and the other items I'd been sent on a sheet of paper, add the Persian-calendar date and put my fingerprint on it before returning to the cell. It is a bit like Christmas: there are some detective novels in English, a book of *Irish Times* Simplex crosswords, socks, an Iranian (fake) Gucci sweatshirt, a blanket, notepads, pencils and an eraser. On Justin's list of items, which should be in the package, I can see that I've also been sent gloves, scarves, woollen hats and hot water bottles, but these must have been impounded. Back in the cell, I learn that all these items are banned in prison. The scarves I can understand, because they could be used to commit suicide or to strangle someone, but banning the rest I find baffling.

Chapter 13

Death Row

It's now November. Every day, I wake up wishing I could speak immediately to Roland, to my family and my friends. Since my first call last week, I've discovered the regulation for calls to family outside Iran is, on paper, one phone call a week. But this is regularly not the case. We can't make external calls from the phones we use during yard time, which are for Iranian numbers only. External calls must be arranged and are monitored.

Iran is either three and a half or four and a half hours ahead of Ireland (the half-hour is so as not to be in the same time zone as Israel). On Sunday mornings at around 11 o'clock, Benjamin usually calls down on the intercom to the guards' office, asking when we can talk to our families. They hardly ever call back. Benjamin continues to call down every twenty or thirty minutes. The tension for the two of us is always terrible. Sometimes we're told that the line isn't working, that there's nobody in security to supervise our calls, or that the phone bill hasn't been paid for that line.

I always get very wound up waiting. Every time I hear someone in the corridor, I wonder if they are coming to get us for our calls. If and when Benjamin is finally brought out for his call, I know that I'm next. I start worrying about getting through to someone; if there's no reply, will I have time to try another number? I'm allowed a call to one of three pre-requested numbers: my father, Roland and my sister, Caroline. So when it's my turn, I try my father's mobile number first. It's too complicated and stressful to ask him to wait for my call at a certain time, so it's always a surprise if he answers. When I can't reach him, I phone Roland or Caroline. Once back in our cell, Benjamin and I always compare notes about what is happening in France and Ireland. His sister, Blandine, is usually able to organise a conference call via Skype, so on his one call he can talk to his mother and other members of his family and even speak to his friends.

This afternoon, under a blue sky, Benjamin and I have a walk in the courtyard. Suddenly we start to sing, loudly, much to the amusement of the other prisoners. We sing the 'Marseillaise', the French national anthem, at the top of our voices. Neither of us knows the exact words but it's great fun. Then we are told over the loudspeaker to stop singing. When our break period is up, we go to the guards' office to ask what the problem is. The guard tells us that he doesn't mind us singing, but not to do so at the far end of the yard because he's trying to sleep.

I realise what this courtyard reminds me of: Kilmainham Gaol in Dublin, which is now a museum. In the courtyard at Kilmainham, crosses mark the place where the revolutionaries of the 1916 Easter Rising were executed. Mashad's high, ominous walls are patrolled along their tops by a guard with a machine gun over his shoulder. He usually waves and shouts a greeting to us. Is it because we are mostly political prisoners rather than common criminals, I wonder.

In the courtyard there are sometimes poor ladybirds on the ground among the dead cockroaches. Today, Benjamin and I put the ladybirds in the flowerbed at one end of the yard.

The yard is under the flight path of the planes taking off from Mashhad airport. As I watch them overhead, I try to imagine flying to freedom. Sometimes I can make out the airline logo, such as Iran Air, Caspian Airlines, Qatar Airways or Mahan Air. The last one I saw today was owned by the Guardians of the Revolution.

5 November. This morning I am brought to the medical centre, to a very large room where there are about five or six people sitting behind desks. Dr Honey is there wearing a big smile. In front of him is a cardboard box bearing a red, white and blue sticker with the words CENTRE DE CRISE (the Crisis Centre at the French Ministry of Foreign Affairs) marked on it. My medication has arrived at last! My doctor in Paris, Dr Pauline Campa, has sent a prescription. A copy in Persian, typed up by the French embassy, is there too. With Dr Honey, I check the contents in the box against the list and give my inked fingerprint as per protocol. Apparently, nothing is missing.

Dr Honey sets aside certain medications, explaining that I will have to come to the medical centre each morning for some of my tablets. I take the rest back to my cell. There I discover that every package has been neatly opened and checked before it reached me.

I've got into a certain habit: after putting my fingerprint on one of the various collection forms, I then rub my inked finger down the ridge of my nose. This look shocked the other prisoners at first, but it's become one of my

106

trademarks. I want to show them that I'm not afraid of being told off by the prisoner workers or guards. I've become known in the block for my pranks and sense of humour. I am innocent and I want people to see my character rather than regarding me as just another prisoner.

Karim, Morthasa and The Dog go to the prison gym every few days. Benjamin and I are not allowed because the authorities don't want their precious merchandise getting damaged, which is a real pain for us. As bargaining tools for the Iranian state, we have to be kept in good condition. I also have trouble with the prison library. Taj says that there are some Persian–English dictionaries there. I fill in a form asking to borrow one, because all we have are French–Persian and English–Persian dictionaries and I'd like to learn a bit of Persian. I never get them. I suspect it's part of our jailers' attempts at mental torture to not allow us to interact more with the Iranians. Taj told me they have refused him books on psychology. However, he has been able to exchange books with other prisoners with the help of the prisoner workers.

9 November. This evening, the three public phone lines were cut. This happens occasionally when someone is to be executed after the call to prayer the next morning – the authorities do not want the condemned person's family to have any foreknowledge of the execution. During our evening kitchen break, I go along the corridor to see the two cells of the condemned men. There are three pairs of flip-flops lined up in front of the doors. The bottom hatches are open and I can hear a man crying inside. It's heart-rending. The fact that the prisoners have no final chance to see their families makes me feel desolate.

13 November. My sixty-fourth birthday. I cry a little in my bunk this morning. It's the first important date since my imprisonment. I think of Roland and my family who must, like me, have woken feeling sad. We cannot even talk directly to one another; it's horrible. But I might be out of this by Christmas. Maybe someone in the regime will realise that I am going to be a headache for them, in particular because of my poor health, and, as a goodwill gesture, they will release me in time for Christmas or the New Year.

15 November. Today, we are prevented from leaving the courtyard after our period outside. The gate back into the block is closed. This is done when they are bringing prisoners who are going to be executed to the cells at the end of the corridor. They do not want them to be seen by other inmates.

During a phone call with the French embassy in Iran, Benjamin and I are told by the consul in Tehran that if all goes to plan, we shall have a consular visit in three days' time. Christian Furceri, the consul, will be coming with the new French ambassador to Iran, Nicolas Roche, who arrived in Tehran on 4 November. It's always last minute with the Iranian authorities and they can also cancel at the last minute, or not allow diplomats to meet us. Benjamin has submitted his written letters to the security people in the prison, so that they might be cleared in time for the visit, but there is no guarantee of this.

The consular visits are usually in the morning. The ambassador and the consul will fly up and the chauffeur will drive, separately, the 1,000 kilometres from Tehran to Mashhad with books and other items sent from France.

The chauffeur will also bring back all the books Benjamin and I have read for other prisoners, as well as Benjamin's finished leather work. We are both excited because we will have news that cannot be given over the phone and there will be a delivery of presents from family and friends, as well as essentials from Tehran, such as good toothpaste and skin cream (everyone in the cell has skin problems because of the very dry atmosphere).

This evening, when the medication is handed out, I take the bottle of Laroxyl that's to help me sleep and pour the drops into a glass of water. When I get past five drops, the nurse and prison worker try to grab the bottle. I ask Taj to explain to them that, on the prescription, translated into Persian, it is marked that I can take between five and twenty drops. The nurse does not appear very reassured.

16 November. I get my debit card at last, so I can feel more financially independent from Benjamin. In fact, I can start buying things for both of us. Roland has to transfer money to a designated French government account first, then the embassy transfers it to my prison account. The amount put on my credit card can never exceed 1,000,000 rials (about €20) or the transaction will not go through, and we are not permitted to have more than 6,000,000 rials in our account at any time. Still, getting the debit card will make a big difference. It also means that I feel like a fully fledged prisoner, with all the accoutrements.

These days, around nine o'clock every morning, I am taken to the medical centre, in another part of the prison, by Hussein. I am brought to a room with a long queue of prisoners outside waiting to enter. Everyone always stares at me in my gold-coloured waistcoat. I say 'salaam' and

109

smile. We foreign prisoners are given priority, so we enter ahead of the others. There are male nurses and equipment for dealing with the day-to-day patching up of injured prisoners: stitching up cuts from fights, handing out medication for various conditions, as well as giving injections, an Iranian speciality. Where in France or Ireland we would swallow medicine such as vitamin D, in Iran they inject it.

Hussein goes to a glass-doored cupboard and takes out a bag with my antidepressant medication, Citalopram, in it. I swallow the tablets in front of him. He then goes to a ledger to note this and the time. The staff at the medical centre usually smile and shake my hand.

Today, I have to wait around because Hussein has another errand. I noticed that some of the prisoners are very old. I see one old man with Parkinson's disease. What has he done to be in prison, I wonder.

Hussein returns with a bag of medication for the prisoners in our block. These include the local version of paracetamol, a small pink tablet that I have taken from time to time for the pain in my back and knees.

This morning Benjamin spoke to his lawyer, Ms Halami, and she has got permission to come and visit us in a few days' time. He speaks to Ms Halami frequently on the phone. His letters home, which are very long, are all posted to her for scanning and then emailed to Benjamin's sister, Blandine, who circulates the letters back in France. Blandine is in very regular contact with the lawyer and the French Ministry of Foreign Affairs.

All forms of contact between Mashhad and the outside world are erratic and unreliable; you always have to go through several channels of mediation and censorship. This extends to letters. There's no set procedure for sending letters home. Benjamin explained to me when I first arrived that we must submit letters to security, with money and instructions to post them, either to Ms Halami in Tehran for Benjamin or, in my case, to Justin Ryan, the Irish chargé d'affaires in Tehran. The diplomats then scan and email the letters to our families. I used this method at the beginning of my confinement, but it took over four weeks for my letters just to get through security. From then on, I gave up and now I dictate my messages over the phone. I prepare my messages in my cell, which I then dictate to Justin and also to Ahmeneh, the French consul's assistant at the French embassy in Tehran, when I have the opportunity. I write many short replies to the dozens of messages I'm getting from all over. Then I write longer messages back to Roland, to Caroline and to my father.

I'm surprised that I haven't heard from certain friends or relatives. Are they afraid, or embarrassed? Do they not know about my imprisonment, or do they not care? Meanwhile, I'm getting messages from people I have not heard from for over thirty years, as well as people I did not expect to hear from, such as my electrician, Philippe.

The emotions I go through dictating my replies are very different, depending on who is on the other end of the phone line. Ahmeneh is incredibly patient, and her tone is so comforting that I sometimes break down in tears while dictating to her.

18 November. Today marks the visit of the diplomats. Benjamin and I are called out of the cell. We give back two bags of books and Benjamin's finished leather work. The books are for four other French prisoners: Luis, Cécile and Jacques in Evin prison in Tehran (like our prison in

Mashhad, Evin has a block for women) and Olivier in Shiraz, a large city about 920 kilometres south of Tehran. The books are examined before we leave our block. We are taken to the clothes check, where the bags are inspected once more. From there, we are taken to part of the prison I have never visited before, near the public entrance. We pass window displays of what the prisoners make: wood-work, leather goods, metalwork, clothes. We go up a flight of stairs and are shown into a warm room with a big conference table. A tall, well-dressed man, in a grey suit and a smart tie (the Iranian regime does not approve of ties, regarding them as a decadent western symbol) approaches us with a big smile. It's Nicolas Roche, the new French ambassador. He hugs both of us. I have trouble holding back my tears. It's also a first for Benjamin; the previous ambassador never visited him. We are then intro-duced to the consul, Christian Furceri, who is more casually dressed, quite a contrast to Roche. On a table beside the diplomats are bags of things for us, mostly books, but also clothes, toothbrushes and skin cream. Benjamin has also got letters.

We gather round the table, with a guard sitting in the corner, holding his mobile phone. I assume he is recording everything and watching our every move. We guess the room is bugged too, so we talk mostly in whispers, or sometimes Roche writes a note to us and passes it across the table. He talks to us in turn. In my case, he tells me about his meetings with Justin and other Irish diplomats. I learn that the Irish government sent a high-level team out from Dublin to Tehran as soon as they learned about my arrest. This included the deputy secretary general in the Department of Foreign Affairs, Sonja Hyland.

A guard comes in with a thermos of hot water for tea, china cups and foil-wrapped biscuits.

'Look, for the time being, we have to keep a low profile and not upset the Iranians,' Roche explains to Benjamin and me.

'Why?'

He adds that they could cut off our communications with our families and/or refuse consular or lawyer visits.

'Look, if it becomes public knowledge that they've cut communications for an ill and innocent hostage, surely their image in the West will be even more tarnished? All that I've got is the fact that I'm older and in poor health – and gay,' I argue.

We agree to differ. Roche tells us that he requested a meeting with the director of the prison and the director of security. The latter has agreed to meet him. The former is not available.

A man from security, dressed in a dark suit that is too big for him, walks in and announces that our time is up. We hand over all the bags brought from Tehran so that the security services can check them. They will take over four weeks to clear everything. Warm hugs with everyone and then back to our cell.

Engaging with the Iranian legal system from inside Mashhad prison is riddled with complexities and inconsistencies. It is gradually confirmed that, as I suspect, the Iranian legal system is a joke. The authorities do not even respect their own rules when it comes to political or security cases.

Benjamin is being defended by Ms Halami, a Tehran-based lawyer who has been involved in a number of cases similar to ours. He suggests that I ask her to help me because she knows the officials at the French embassy and, above all, she has the mobile numbers of the top brass in the prison. I add Ms Halami's mobile number to my phone card (but when Benjamin talks to her, he usually passes me over to her so as not to use up an extra call allowance). She agrees to defend me, but then explains that the authorities would first have to agree to her involvement.

♠ ♠ ♠

It's been a few days since the diplomats' visit, and today we have a meeting with Ms Halami, who has agreed to represent me. Instead of the pleasant, warm room we occupied for the consular visit, this meeting is held in a freezing room, again near the entrance. A guard sits at the table with the three of us. Ms Halami is a small, slight woman, probably in her fifties. She is well wrapped up, unlike Benjamin and me, who are frozen in our stockinged feet and flip-flops. We have brought Benjamin's French–Persian dictionary in case we need it.

Ms Halami explains to Benjamin how his case is proceeding through the Iranian legal system, with its myriad layers, from lower to middle courts up to the supreme court. For my case, she is waiting to know if the court will allow her to defend me. She was at the court in Mashhad earlier this morning but was not allowed to see anything about my case. (I later discovered that the courts hardly ever send any documents to the accused's lawyer.) Nonetheless, Ms Halami has had to make a 2,000-kilometre return trip in order to attend the court. She was not allowed to photocopy or photograph the documents but had to write out copies of everything in longhand.

At one stage, we have to look up a word in the dictionary, which we show to Ms Halami. The guard asks to see the word but makes no comment when we show it to him. Eventually our time is up, and we are brought back to our cell.

I'm disheartened by the encounter, but then I get a message from Roland, who tells me that all the work I did pruning our olive trees in Banyuls-sur-Mer appears to have paid off. I worked hard in early 2022, after completing a two-week course at an agricultural college in Nîmes, pruning the trees, which had been abandoned for about five years. Roland says that all the trees I worked on have a lot of fruit and they have not been attacked by the olive fly (I hung out over seventy traps for this pest). Sadly, I am not going to be there for my first winter harvest.

Chapter 14

Winter in Mashhad

21 November. I have asked to see Dr Honey because I can no longer sleep. I explained the situation and asked him for something really strong to knock me out at night because of the constant noise and light in the cell. Last night, I was given three red tablets, one white tablet and some white powder, which I downed with a glass of water. I had trouble staying awake for the last roll call at 10 p.m. Once in bed, I was fast asleep in a few minutes. This morning, I had no problem getting up, which cheers me up because sleep is my only escape from this living nightmare. It looks as if the tablets will work well.

It is getting cold in the cell: the windows let in draughts and the big fans in the toilet area suck out whatever warm air there is. There are three small radiators which are, at best, warm, in the morning and evening, like the hot water for the shower. In addition, two of them are hidden behind bunk beds, which is not great for heating the cell. So I've copied the way my cellmates get round the problem: Coca-Cola bottles! We fill the large plastic bottles with hot water; not too hot or the bottle will melt. I always put a little cold water in first, just in case. I have three large

Coke bottles and two small Sprite bottles in my bed now. Everyone spends most of the day in bed.

Benjamin and I send written complaints to the prison authorities, warning them that because of our fragile health, we could fall seriously ill and that if that happened, it would be their fault.

23 November. When I get through to Justin Ryan on the phone today, he reads out a letter from the Irish Minister of Foreign Affairs, Micheál Martin, who is also the Tánaiste (Ireland's deputy prime minister). Mr Martin explains in his letter that his departmental officials are working hard to get me out of prison and that everyone in government is pushing to have my case resolved.

When I tell Benjamin about this, he says that he has *never* got a letter from the French government. Seeing that the Irish authorities are so concerned about me makes him a bit jealous.

This same evening, Ms Halami informs me on the phone that the court does not recognise her as my lawyer. I am not too upset, because I know already that I am not going to get out of prison via the 'due process' of the Iranian legal system. Later, while Benjamin and I are walking in the yard, we are called to the guards' office. There, a tall man in a well-cut beige suit is sitting with a number of guards. Benjamin knows Mr Houey well because he was just a guard when Benjamin arrived two and a half years ago and since then he has moved up through the ranks of the security service. He speaks French and, according to Benjamin, some Japanese (Benjamin had worked in Japan for a short spell).

'Bernard, why do you put so much detail in your letters about life in prison?' Mr Houey asks me.

117

'I want people to understand what life is like here,' I say. 'I haven't talked about the other prisoners or about my own health,' I add. I go on to tell him that I have not been able to talk to my father once since my arrest and that tomorrow, 24 November, is his 97th birthday and that I am always in Dublin on this, his special day.

At this, Mr Houey stands up and he, Benjamin and I go to the yard and walk up and down, much to the stupefaction of our cellmates who, like us, are on their morning break. In a low voice, Mr Houey says to me, 'There's no case against you. You shouldn't be in prison'.

I'm taken aback at the directness but use the opportunity to remind him that my health is declining and that I am not sure how much more of this detention I can take. My blood pressure is sky high and my eyesight is getting worse.

'I'll try to find out more about your case,' he offers.

'I really want to call my father,' I add. 'I just want to wish him a happy birthday.'

'I'll do my best,' he says.

24 November. This morning we ask the security services about making a phone call. As usual, they say that they will get back to us. During our morning cell break, Mr Houey appears again in the courtyard. He tells me that the bill for that phone line has not been paid by the prison authorities. I am downcast. Does this mean that calling families is going to get even more complicated? I ask him why my family cannot phone me, like Benjamin's family does him. Mr Houey says that it is out of his control, before walking out of the courtyard and returning a few minutes later, smiling broadly. 'I have solved the problem,' he says, and asks me to come with him right away. As we pass through the security office, his colleagues look on and I can tell that they respect Mr Houey. When we reach the phone area, he says that I can call my father.

After just two or three rings, I hear the sound of the receiver being lifted and then the familiar voice. 'Hello?'

Tears roll down my cheeks. My father is crying too. 'How are you holding up?' he asks me. 'Are you taking your medication?'

'Oh, yes,' I reply vaguely. I don't want to worry him with the truth. I think about him sitting in his living room at home in Dublin, the phone to his ear, while I'm standing thousands of miles away in prison.

'What are the conditions like in the prison?' he asks. 'Is the food terrible?'

'Not bad,' I reassure him. Mr Houey is sitting opposite me and understands every word I am speaking. I talk about everyday things and say I hope to be home for Christmas. The call has boosted my morale. My father sounds well and alert. I am so relieved.

26 November. The football World Cup in Qatar started last week. The Iranians are football fanatics, so we are allowed to have the television on later in the evening. I am not a football fan and have never watched a complete football match on television but find that censorship in Iran is used in the most surprising ways. For the opening ceremony, Iranian television cuts to aerial views of the stadium when it's the turn of the Israeli and US teams to parade. It's the same for any problematic pictures of the crowd. Benjamin explains to me that there is a time lapse of about two minutes in the transmission just in case there's a problem, such as the camera zooming in on a scantily clad woman. It makes for some odd cuts in the coverage.

Before each match, the politicians and commentators always say, like most people in Iran, 'Inshallah', which means 'God willing', regarding a possible win for Iran, who have qualified for the World Cup. Then when the team loses, they say it's a mistake. Benjamin and I like to tease the Iranians about this.[1]

When the French are playing, it's sometimes very late. Normally, the television would be off, but some of the guards leave it on for us. The next day we thank them: it means that we can take our mind off things, for this month at least. Yellow Vest tries to stir up trouble with Benjamin and me by saying there are no 'real' Frenchmen on the team. We both point out that practically all the players were born in France and that this is also the case in most countries, where racial minorities are present in every walk of life. I wanted to say, but refrained, that the Irish prime minister, Leo Varadkar, is gay, lives with another man, and is half-Indian. In Iran, it is almost impossible to be gay. In fact, rather than face this fact, the government subsidises transgender surgery for men who are, in fact, gay.

---

[1] Benjamin and I did not know while we were in prison, but we later found out that the Iranian team had refused to sing the country's national anthem at their opening game. A very popular player, 26-year-old Amir Nasr-Azadani, who was not selected for the World Cup squad, spoke out about the women-led protests, and was arrested in December 2022 in Isfahan. He was sentenced in January 2024 to 26 years in prison. Many members of the Iranian team play in clubs in Europe. One player who plays for a German team flew directly to Qatar so that he did not have to meet the Iranian president, Ebrahim Raisi, in Tehran.

28 November. Today there is a documentary about Hitler on the television. Iran had a very ambiguous relationship with German fascism, perhaps influenced by the regime's anti-Jewish position. Yellow Vest is sitting on the floor in the middle of the room watching the television programme while I am sitting on the floor by my bunk reading a book. Suddenly he turns to me and says that he admires Hitler. I am dumbstruck.

Chapter 15

The Month Before Christmas

4 December. It is getting colder all the time – a dry, penetrating, inescapable cold that seems to enter my bones. We have seen reports on television of heavy snowfalls in other parts of Iran. Today we had our first snow shower. I like the way the snowflakes drift towards the earth and decorate the coils of barbed wire on the security fences with a froth of white lace.

Prison workers came to the cell this morning to seal up the windows with plaster, a barrier against the terrible draughts. They have reduced most of the draughts, but the panes of glass are so thin, it's still bitterly cold in the cell. The TV news has been showing scenes of chaos across the country: it's so cold that the diesel in train locomotives has frozen. There are problems with the gas network, so the time we are allowed to cook has been reduced. And the temperatures keep on falling.

7 December. Today is the coldest day in Mashhad for years. Most of us have stayed in bed fully dressed, getting up only for meals or to pour fresh hot water into our empty Coke bottles. I long for my woollen hat and gloves that have been impounded. I am starting to feel really depressed and miserable, thinking that nothing will ever happen towards my release. The idea of spending years in here, like Benjamin, is unthinkable. In bed, I have got into the habit of turning towards the wall and crying.

More sad news has come: Taj's father has died and he is not allowed to attend the funeral in his home town. Taj doesn't say anything immediately, but he has been very quiet and his eyes are red. Earlier, he called me over, saying he wanted to show me something. He pulled a picture of an old man smiling at the camera out of a book. It is his father. It makes me wonder if my dad will be alive when I get out, whenever that might be. All this makes me very sad.

This evening, I decide to fill in a form complaining about the way the prison lies to us. I point out that lying in Islam and in Christian religions is supposed to be a bad thing. So why, when we ask for something like a phone call with our families, or for a book from the prison library, are we told yes, and then nothing happens? I point out that surely this will not be good for the believer in the afterlife. I know very well nobody is going to reply, but it gets something off my chest that really annoys me. Why can they not just say 'no'?

It's probably part of the practice of doing everything possible to create a bad atmosphere in the prison. For example, never allowing us out of our cell on time. Sometimes they can be twenty minutes late. But the only time they are late getting us back to our cell is when a poor man is being put in the holding cell before execution the next morning, because they don't want us to see him.

8 December. Today I decide to cheer everyone up with some European cooking. I have previously cooked stuffed peppers using the prison's supply of cooked rice. Now, Ahmeneh in the French embassy has given me a recipe for orange crumble over the phone, so I decide to try that. In our cell we have a huge pot that serves as an oven, about 50 centimetres in diameter and 20 centimetres deep. About six kilos of salt are put in the bottom. Then I place the orange crumble in a dish on the bed of salt and seal the lid with a damp newspaper. The pot goes on the gas ring in the kitchen, with another pot full of water placed on top to reinforce the seal.

Because Benjamin has his leather workshop near the kitchen, he can turn off the gas when the dish is cooked. It works well. The rancid butter really doesn't taste too bad and there are grateful smiles from my cellmates when they have eaten their fill.

Taj has shown me how to make saffron tea. He grinds the filaments with a little sugar, then adds boiling water. Not much is needed to fill a thermos of this delicious reddish drink. It makes a welcome change from the monotony of black prison tea.

10 December. I am taken to see Dr Honey this morning. He is very concerned about my high blood pressure and says that, from now on, it will need to be taken every evening. While I am sitting in his office, a prisoner appears at the door, screaming in pain, blood streaming from a big cut on his head. He is whisked away, leaving a trail of blood behind him. The weapon that has inflicted the injury was almost certainly made inside the prison by another inmate: by breaking a disposable razor and putting the blade between two telephone cards, you can create a lethal weapon.

15 December. My visits to the medical centre every evening for blood pressure readings have brought me into contact with a new group of prisoners. There is a diabetic man in his sixties, with only one arm, who speaks excellent English, with an American accent. He was a lawyer but has been imprisoned for the murder of a woman, I think in Mashhad. I lend him a Richard Osman Thursday Murder Club novel. He does not comment on my choice but does not ask for more books.

My blood pressure reading is too high, and the nurse isn't happy. Unknown to anyone, I am not taking the tablets for my blood pressure, which I am allowed to keep in the cell. I throw them down the toilet every morning. I want to show the authorities that I am unwell and that keeping me in prison is not a good idea. My ill health is my immediate objective to get me out of this mess.

16 December. The regional newspaper that Taj gets delivered every day has stopped coming without explanation. It was already censored, with pages regularly missing. It is popular with the political prisoners because there is lots of local news in it, as well as the television listings, a crossword and Sudoku. Benjamin and I never see any newspapers.

This afternoon, we are in the corridor downstairs when we bump into Morthasa, our young cellmate from Torbat. He's well dressed and carrying a bag. He's being released! It is a very emotional moment for Karim, Taj and Benjamin, because Morthasa had been there for a while. I didn't know him well. The Iranians just shake hands with Morthasa as they say goodbye. No hugs.

18 December. Today, the Football World Cup ends. Benjamin was supposed to have been managing two of the host playing grounds in Qatar instead of languishing here with me. He worries a lot about what his future might be like once he gets out of prison. There is going to be a rather large gap in his CV.

20 December. I get to talk to Roland today, who is with friends at our house in Banyuls-sur-Mer. They are helping with the renovation. We know the area very well because we had a house in a nearby village, Cerbère, for twelve years, before moving to Banyuls three years ago. Other friends are helping to cut down dead trees and clear the undergrowth.

Later, Benjamin and I are called down to security. Mr Houey is there, well dressed as usual. It is so warm in the security offices, he is in his short-sleeved shirt. He has a hardback copy of *Don Quixote* (which, I learned later, Cervantes wrote in prison), which I had asked Justin Ryan to send me. Houey explains that it is too big and that he can't give it to me. I reply that I have no intention of hitting anyone with it. He says that isn't the problem: such a thick book can be hollowed out in order to circulate objects between prisoners, just like in the movies. Everyone laughs and Houey then passes me the book. However, he will not give me the woollen hats that Justin has also sent. I point out that some prisoners have made their own hats and there seems to be no problem with that, but he won't change his mind.

We go back to our cell with our arms full of things. Since I now have plenty of socks, I've given the new pairs to Benjamin, Karim, Reswan and Taj.

21 December. This afternoon, we get a new cellmate, a Kuwaiti in his twenties. He's here because an Iranian woman accused him of touching her in the bazaar. He explained that he was visiting Mashhad with his girlfriend and that he did not touch the woman. I learned that this is a ploy that women in Mashhad use on foreign men. To get out of prison, the Kuwaiti has to pay the woman a fine, fixed by her and her family.

Yellow Vest is very friendly with the new arrival. He gives presents to all new arrivals. I got a pair of socks when I was first imprisoned. He cooks a meal for the new guest this evening. I think Yellow Vest hopes that once the Kuwaiti is released, he can persuade him to send him money.

23 December. There is a change of prisoner manager today. (This is a prisoner who manages the other prison workers in each block.) It turns out the previous guy had been cooking the books in the shop. The new guy, with lots of tattoos on his arms, comes into the cell with his cronies. He is not a pleasant guy and he does not say hello to Benjamin or me. There's a lot of tension among the prison workers.

We go to the barber's for a haircut. Marchmout is the man who cuts prisoners' hair. He's also an excellent cook. There is always another prison worker sitting there as well. I'm not sure exactly why, maybe to make sure a pair of scissors is not taken. Benjamin and I pay for Reswan's haircut because he has so little money. I tip Marchmout with a bar of chocolate. The new prisoner manager is at the hairdresser's at least twice a week. He never has a hair out of place.

25 December. Christmas passes and no phone calls are allowed. Benjamin and I don't even discuss the festival because it's too painful. I am really down in the dumps. At least there are no Christmas programmes on the television. It's very difficult not to think about family back in Ireland and France. This Christmas, I had planned to bring my father to France for probably his last visit. At 97, he's finding it increasingly difficult to get about. It would have been good for him to enjoy some French food and wine in sunny Banyuls-sur-Mer.

28 December. Early this morning, the door slid open and in came prison workers and two 'outside' workers. We are told they are going to install an extra camera in the cell and change the old one. They want to remove two sets of bunk beds because the cameras cannot see everyone properly. The bunks in question belong to Taj and Karim, who have to move. The shelves beneath the television are also to be removed. So, with very noisy tools, they proceed to cut up the bunks and shelves.

Dara, an Irish friend back in Paris, sent me earplugs and eye masks to help me sleep. I never wear the latter because they bring back too many bad memories of being blindfolded; none of the political prisoners wanted them either. But I am now able to pass out my spare earplugs. There is dust everywhere. It's a great opportunity to clean the cell afterwards. A vacuum cleaner is brought up by the prison workers and almost everyone gets involved in cleaning and reorganising the cell. Poor Taj has to find room for the things he has accumulated over his seven years inside.

31 December. New Year's Eve. I cried a little today, wondering when this nightmare is going to end.

Chapter 16

Hunger Strike

3 January 2023. Benjamin went on hunger strike early in his imprisonment and the idea has been going round in my head for a while. So this morning I fill in a form indicating that I am going on hunger strike and refusing to take my medication. At the first break, I go to the guards' office and hand in the form and my bag of medication. The guards don't want to take the bag at first, but I put it on the ground so they know that I'm serious. I feel a weight coming off my shoulders. I phone Ahmeneh and Justin to let them know. I know that it is going to cause trouble back home, but I want to make the Iranians even more concerned about my health.

Back in the cell, I drink tea with sugar for the first time in years. I also use tomato purée dissolved in hot water to make sure I am getting enough salt.

10 January. I have refused to go to the medical centre this morning, but I continue to go every evening for my blood pressure reading, with the expectation that the prison authorities will worry about my health. Yesterday, when I arrived, a prisoner was handcuffed to a stretcher and a nurse and a guard were trying to hold him down and give him an injection, which he obviously did not want. He was screaming. Another nurse arrived and took my blood pressure; it was even higher than usual. He started shouting at me in English about taking my medication and about the hunger strike. He went away and came back with a tablet, which he wanted me to put under my tongue. I refused. He got angry and explained the problem to the prison worker. I said, 'When I am freed from this hole, I will take my medication again.'

The nurse came back with me to my cell. He talked to Benjamin, who knew all about my plans and who just shrugged and continued reading his book. The nurse and prison worker went out and a few minutes later, the guard on duty came to the cell and shouted at me. I ignored him. He's really not happy. My strategy seems to be working.

11 January. I recently asked Benjamin if he can teach me some leather work, because the marking and stitching can be done in the cell. During our hour and a half cooking break, I join Benjamin in his workshop, where I can sit in a chair. Bliss. Each time he goes to his workshop, he has to collect his tools from the guards' office. These include cutters, scissors and other sharp instruments for punching holes in the leather. Even the used blades from the cutter must be accounted for. Benjamin is able to buy leather from outside the prison with the help of one of the guards. He has a huge quantity of cow, sheep and camel skins. Most have been tanned in various colours.

Benjamin starts me off with a small rectangular bag. Using a template, he cuts out the various pieces for me and shows me how to use a special ruler and pen to mark where the holes have to be punched.

The arrival of a new leather worker has amused everyone. Hussein, who usually takes me to the medical centre, and Hassan, another prison worker, also do leather work. A popular item to make is a small wallet to hold our phone and debit cards. Often, prisoners will order an item from a catalogue to give a relative when they visit. I hear that prison workers are used as cheap labour by outside companies, but I don't know if this is true. Even the guards order work from Benjamin, such as repairing the binding of one of their ledgers. It's good fun as we chat away while the others cook or phone their families. Before I arrived, Benjamin's diet, apart from the prison food, was mainly fried eggs. Thanks to my cooking and to Taj's, he began to eat more fresh vegetables, like tomatoes and aubergines. Now that I am no longer eating, he has returned to his old diet.

12 January. My hunger strike continues. It's been nine days. At first, it was difficult to see and smell food. My stomach rumbles a lot. I drink more tea and tomato purée in water to try to compensate for the lack of food. I read more, too, trying to forget that I am hungry. After the first few days it has become easier, but my energy has faded and I take longer to walk anywhere.

One of the prison workers, Hassan – in prison for having set up a home laboratory making drugs – is good-looking and very good friends with Benjamin and me. I am convinced he's gay. He's always trying to arrange things for us. For example, we ask him to see if there are books and parcels in security for us. He is able to move around the whole prison, so he can get messages to other prisoners, too. Security is so strict that it's complicated to move things. One day, a prisoner was coming into our block as I was waiting to go to the medical block. The guard came out and took the packet of cigarettes from the prisoner and examined the tip of each cigarette to see if there were drugs hidden in them.

Messages are starting to arrive from family and friends, asking me to stop my hunger strike. I even get a message from a client and friend, Carole Adam, in Paris, who is angry with me for embarking on a hunger strike. I explain, in messages dictated to Ahmeneh, that this is the only weapon I have to try to get out of this place. I tell them that I am fully aware of the risks, but the idea of being locked up for years is something I cannot cope with.

13 January. We receive a second consular visit from Nicolas Roche and Christian Furceri, the consul. Christian is a keen woodworker and Benjamin told me that his landlord in Tehran was so surprised to see all his equipment, including electric saws, that he asked Furceri if he was a carpenter.

Again, there's an exchange of books and presents from home for both of us. I would love to receive letters as Benjamin does. That way I could read them again and again, instead of having them read to me over the phone. Roche is very concerned about my hunger strike and asks me to stop. I explain that I cannot until I am released, and if the Iranians want to see me returning to France on a stretcher, it will be their fault. I point out to Roche that a hunger strike is an Irish speciality that goes back to the 1920s and the fight for independence. In fact, the Iranians changed the street name in Tehran where the British embassy is located from Winston Churchill Boulevard to

Bobby Sands Street after the IRA hunger striker, who died in 1981. As a consequence, the British had to move the entrance to the embassy to a side street to avoid using the new address.

14 January. Today, there is no gas. This is a country with some of the biggest natural gas reserves in the world. So, no hot water for showers and the prison food is barely lukewarm, although my cellmates continue to eat it.

I spoke to Furceri this morning. He read me a message from Roland, before passing me to Ahmeneh, so that I could dictate messages to her. She asks me if Furceri has read the messages from Roland to me. I reply that there is only one. Ahmeneh tells me that there are, in fact, three messages from Roland. She reads me the other two. (On my return to Europe, I was to discover that lots of messages had never reached me. My godchild, Léopold, had three times sent me poems he'd written. I never got one. I sometimes wondered if someone was censoring my messages.)

18 January. This morning, Justin Ryan reads me a message from my father, pleading with me to give up my hunger strike. I discuss it with Benjamin and decide to formally tell the prison authorities that I am going to eat and take my medication, at my father's request.

It's been two weeks, but I think I could have gone on for a fair bit longer. I am not sure what the prison authorities would have done. They would probably have put me in hospital and force-fed me, but the news of me in hospital and getting force-fed would have been terrible for their image. The Iranians do not want to be seen to be harming Europeans.

19 January. On television we see some of the protests still happening all over the country, which we are told are caused by hooligans with the backing of foreign powers. Every time someone dies in police custody, it's because the person committed suicide or was in poor health. There is plenty of gore on the news, with pictures of the bodies of murdered policemen in their car that has been vandalised by protestors. They even show the police breaking into a flat and violently arresting people. We form the impression that the country is on fire.

One evening, we see and hear fireworks being set off. I learn that this is done by supporters of the protesters in our prison.

Talking to an Iranian prisoner who has just returned from an interrogation centre, I learn that the cells there are crowded with young protesters. He tells me that one protester had a relative in the police and he was told that the police would cut the CCTV cameras in part of the city so that the protesters could not be identified. The policeman was taking a terrible risk.

The prisoners in the interrogation centre cell noticed that they had a sort of rash on their feet. Was something put in the drinking water? I remembered my rash in the interrogation centre and having only tap water to drink.

Chapter 17

The Revolutionary Court

20 January. Last night, after the last roll call, a prison worker handed a blue-striped prisoner uniform into the cell for me. The uniform is, in part, a message: I would be going to court the next morning. The last-minute reveal is intentional and routine, so that prisoners do not phone their families or lawyers to warn them, despite reasonable notice being a requirement of Iranian law. I was very tense as Benjamin sat with me on the floor and explained what was probably going to happen in my first court appearance. I listened patiently as he told me that I would probably be asked to sign some documents, which would be in Persian. I told him I would sign nothing unless my lawyer was present, which was not going to be the case.

This morning, Benjamin has my breakfast ready as I get dressed. I put a T-shirt on under the uniform top and a pair of socks. Being January, it is cold at 6 a.m.

A prison worker brings me downstairs to the guards' office. There I wait while a chit is written and a phone call made for someone to come and collect me. The prisoners from other blocks are able to make their own way to the first checkpoint, but the tenants of block 6-1 are always escorted, possibly because the authorities are worried that they might communicate with other prisoners. Being passed from one official to the next at each stage in the maze-game of Mashhad is part of the routine.

My collector brings me down the long corridor, making sure I walk along the side, as per the rules. If I stray towards the centre of the corridor, the guard will gesture to me to get back to the side, so that I know my place. We pass staff and clerics breezing freely down the middle of the corridor as they arrive for work, as well as other prisoners, dressed like me for court appearances, skirting the opposite wall.

At the first checkpoint, we are made to kneel in rows and wait. A guard with a long ledger then calls out our names and, one by one, we go into a room where we have to strip to our underpants. As I emerge, I notice a selection of tattoos on display: animals, Persian writing, faces. Only the likenesses of other men are inked, because images of women are forbidden.

We then go, one by one, into the clothes-check area. Young guards, wearing gloves, take the uniform I have been carrying. One pulls at the elastic of my underpants and motions for me to turn around so he can check if I am hiding anything inside my underwear. I am told to remove my socks: they are not allowed. Another prisoner helps me to place them under the seat of a chair in the room before the checking area. The guard speaks to me in English, asking where I am from and why I am in prison. I reply that I am Irish and that I do not know why I have been imprisoned.

My uniform is handed back and I am shown through another door. Here, a guard with a ledger notes my name and directs me into yet another room with chairs placed around the walls. It seems like a holding pen. From the barred windows I can see a courtyard outside. I am still so cold: there are no heaters in the room. The guards are in their warm office just beside us, drinking tea.

A young prisoner insists that I take his seat because there aren't enough for everyone. We are about fifty men of all ages. A fair few have scarred faces and look particularly nasty, the sort of individuals you would not like to meet on a dark street at night. But then it occurs to me that I am one of them, in a strange way. There is a good deal of chatting, since, for many, this is the only place where they see their pals, because the blocks never mix. There is one dark-haired prisoner with a scar on his cheek and piercing dark eyes who keeps glancing at me unsmilingly. He is clutching documents to his chest.

Eventually, unmarked minibuses start coming into the yard outside and parking in a line. A door opens and a guard, holding another ledger, calls out a name and a figure will move forward, then disappear into the yard.

Out in the cold air, a group of young guards handcuffs us into pairs and puts shackles on each prisoner. Benjamin warned me about these shackles: they can really hurt the ankles. He told me to pull down the legs of my uniform and tuck them inside each shackle to protect my ankles. It works, except for the step up into the minibus. The trouser leg rides up and the cold metal chafes against my freezing foot. As I head for the back seats, others board behind me. Then two guards, one with a machine gun, and an officer with a pistol, come on board. As usual, I am asked where I am from and so on. The guard sitting near me can speak a little English and gives me a sad smile as I tell him my story. He then takes out a sandwich and, to my surprise, gives me half. It's a little warm, and it tastes delicious.

The bus is stopped and we wait as more paperwork is exchanged before we drive out into the morning traffic and the metal gate closes behind us. I've been told to keep the curtains on the windows closed, but I am compelled to peep through to the streets outside. For the first time in months, I can see normal life occurring, men and women going about their lives. It is a weird experience to move through a world I am being kept away from.

We proceed with no accompanying police cars or sirens. Our unmarked vehicles could have been taking excited tourists on an outing. I wish people could see us in our blue-striped uniforms: maybe then they would realise how many prisoners are moving around their city this morning.

As we sit in the heavy traffic, I take in the faces of the people on the pavements, the trees, the buildings and shops and, in the distance, the snow-capped mountains. After about half an hour we turn into a tree-lined street and pull up in front of an office building about five storeys high, surrounded by a high wall. The courthouse. A guard diverts the public from walking on the footpath while we shuffle in our flip-flops and shackles from the minibus, through an entryway in the high wall, to the other side.

There, we are ushered into a small room. The guards have to hand in their ammunition – machine-gun cartridges and pistol bullets – then we're out again, into the court-yard. We make our way to another building around the back and into a hallway. There, the officer details guards to accompany us to various parts of the building. I am to go to the third floor. We are not allowed to take the lift. My handcuffs are removed, but not the shackles, so climbing the stairs proves to be a painful exercise.

When we arrive at the third floor, we face a long, wide corridor with rows of seats and lots of waiting Iranians. I am shown to a seat. Everyone is looking at me because I am the only foreigner. I just smile back to show them that I am just an unlucky European caught up in their struggle for more freedom. I am not a criminal. A woman gets up and asks my guard a question. I don't know what he replies but she shakes her head and goes back to her seat. After a short time, I am brought through an office with veiled secretaries typing on computers and into another room. Here, behind a raised desk, sits the judge. There is no jury in this court, nor any legal representation. Another man presents himself as a translator. He starts to explain, in very broken English, what is going to happen. I tell him I cannot understand what he is talking about. The judge seems to realise what the problem is. I think he understands English, and I am pleased that he sends the guy packing. The judge obviously feels that it is important that I fully understand what is going on. A few minutes later, a replacement translator turns up who can speak far better English.

The judge proceeds to read out the charges against me, which are then translated into English. I have been accused of sending information to an enemy state. I ask the judge if France is an enemy state; he simply replies, 'Not yet.' I deny the charges. A document, in Persian, is put in front of me and I am asked to sign it. I refuse. I ask the judge if he would sign a document in Irish or French. I am so annoyed at his refusal to even respect Iran's own laws regarding prisoners' rights, there is no way I am going to cooperate with him. He insists that I sign, saying that I am only going to make matters worse for myself if I don't.

My assigned guard is called in, and he, too, tries to persuade me to sign the document. I still refuse. I cross my arms and look at the ground. I really want to annoy them and show that I am going to make life difficult for these people. What have I got to lose? I am in serious trouble already, stuck in a prison as a state hostage, thousands of kilometres from family and friends.

Eventually, the judge tells me to leave the room. As I walk out, he calls after me, in English, 'You will die in prison.' The shock of hearing this is terrible. Perhaps my bad health will finish me off in prison, not my prison sentence.

As we go back into the corridor, the guard is shaking his head. From there, instead of going out to the minibus, as I expected, I am brought down to the basement. The guard opens a metal door in the corridor and I am directed into a huge room. It must be about five metres high, and although it has no lighting, it is not dark. With just three windows set very high up in the wall, there is enough light to see other prisoners sitting on the floor. Near the ceiling is a big fan heater, but it's turned off. It's really cold. Three of the prisoners have a clever technique to avoid sitting directly on the cold floor: they each sit on one of their flip-flops and rest their bare feet on the other one. I do the same.

Gradually, other prisoners turn up. It becomes obvious that this is yet another holding area. The dark-haired prisoner with the scar turns up. He comes up to me and says, pointing to himself, 'Daesh' (the Islamic terrorist organisation), drawing a finger across his throat. I just shrug and look away. He comes back to me once or twice repeating 'Daesh'. I pretend not to be intimidated.

More and more prisoners turn up. A young guy, probably in his late teens, comes up and asks me in broken

English where I am from. I ask him why he's in here. He just lifts his right arm and clenches his fist. A protester.

After what seems a long time, a guard comes to the door and says something; another prisoner nods to me and we troop out. The 'Daesh' prisoner is told to stay put. I consider the fact that the Iranian authorities are extremely harsh with any sympathisers of Daesh or ISIS and wonder what might happen to this man. We go back upstairs to the hall, where we are handcuffed once more. We shuffle back out to the office, where the guards are given their ammunition. It is chilling to see the officer putting each bullet back into the cylinder of his pistol. Then it's out to the minibus, past the humiliating stares of the public.

Back at the prison, our handcuffs are removed, but it takes the guards ages to remove the shackles because they have a complicated locking mechanism. In the end, one of the guards gives us a key so we can unlock them ourselves. At the clothes check, the body search is more intrusive than before. The guard asks me to open my mouth and then he runs his gloved finger around my gums. I am also asked to show the soles of my feet in case I am hiding something there.

Despite my fellow prisoner's advice to leave my socks under the seat in the holding cell, they're missing.

It's now early afternoon. Back in the cell, Benjamin has kept me lunch and uses the intercom to ask for someone to come up to get the food reheated. I take a cold shower. There will be no more hot water until 10 p.m.

Benjamin and I try to work out if we've seen the same judge. I tell him about the judge's parting shot that chilled me to the bone.

141

Chapter 18

Benjamin's False Release

28 January. Since early January, Benjamin has been in touch a lot with his lawyer, Ms Halami, because the court in Tehran is reviewing his case. This afternoon, there is an announcement on the cell's loudspeaker: 'Benjamin is free'. There is clapping and cheering from most of the prisoners in the room. Two prison workers come to collect him. He hugs everyone. I feel very sad that I am losing my friend. How will I manage on my own? It will be very difficult not having someone to talk to, to share my stress. Life is going to get more complicated without him, thousands of kilometres from home.

I feel very alone for the first time since arriving in this prison. Benjamin's release will upset my family. They will want to know why I have not been released at the same time. But it might galvanise the authorities in Europe to step up their action to secure my release.

Taj and I divide Benjamin's things between us and the other prisoners. I throw out his toothbrush and hairbrush (Benjamin, in protest at his detention, has not cut his hair since he arrived in prison, much to the anger of the guards. They threaten him regularly with having his head shaved by force).

This same evening, the door opens and in walks Benjamin! To our astonishment, he explains that just before the last gate, where his lawyer would be waiting for him, a guard came up to him and said he had to go back to his cell. Naturally, he is shattered; his eyes are red from tears. Later, he is able to call Ms Halami, but she is just as lost as Benjamin. On paper he is free, but someone does not want him to leave. The guards are very confused because, to them, a free man is in prison and their bureaucracy says nothing about this type of case; therefore, Benjamin has to be guilty of something.

30 January. Today, I hear a new voice on the phone instead of the chargé d'affaires, Justin Ryan. Ronan, from the Irish embassy in Ankara, has been sent to help Justin. He's very interested in Iranian culture and wants to travel. I give him suggestions of places to visit. I am promoting Iran from inside the prison! All I want to do is help the man 'enjoy' his posting.

This evening, a cellmate tells me that he has heard from family that a letter between the Tánaiste, Micheál Martin, and his Iranian counterpart has been leaked to Saudi media. I wonder who's behind this and why. Could it be Iranian opposition outside the country?

1 February. Benjamin tells me that he has decided to go on hunger strike again. He's really cracking up. He does not want to tell the prison authorities though. He says they will learn of it when it's reported by The Dog that he's no longer eating. I disagree. If he formally tells the authorities now, they will know he has also told his family back home and so they cannot deny it.

9 February. This afternoon, Ahmeneh reads me a message from my sister-in-law, Chantal, and her partner, Jean-Pierre, both big rugby fans, with the score in the Six Nations, which apparently has just started. She says that she hopes that I shall be out so that we can watch the last matches together. She goes on to give me the results and a short commentary after every match, much to the amusement of my cellmates. Taj asks his wife on the phone to find out more about this 'strange' sport. I point out that Georgia has a national team that plays regularly in the Rugby World Cup.

10 February. It turns out I am correct: Nicolas Roche tells Benjamin that the prison does not recognise his hunger strike. On top of that, Benjamin is skinny already, so it will not be immediately clear that he has lost weight. The prisoners know, however, that word will spread fast. I now try to eat when Benjamin is not in the cell. It's not always easy because sometimes I eat with the others at the usual mealtimes.

Two Iraqi men have joined us in the cell. Apparently, they are in for some sort of sex scandal. There are amusing negotiations as usual between them and Yellow Vest about making phone calls. Yellow Vest is involved because over time he has been able to acquire multiple phone cards to call various places. There's a technique whereby the person at the other end of the line uses another phone to call a third party, for example in Iraq, and puts the two handsets together so the men in prison can talk to whoever they like. Benjamin and I are not allowed to do this, nor are the diplomatic missions allowed to organise conference calls. This is a pity.

I get a message from my sister, Caroline. The private secretary to the Irish President, Michael D. Higgins, has written to our father regarding my case. According to Benjamin, this is better than he got after three years in prison.

Every now and then there is trouble in the big cell on the other side of our corridor. You can hear the guards coming with prison workers to quieten things down. Or it could be a prisoner protesting because he is being taken from the cell. The metal door in our cell does not close perfectly, so if we kneel, we can see through the gap what's happening in the corridor. But today that comes to an end when a team of prison workers and outside contractors weld a strip of metal to the door frame so we can no longer look out.

I have noticed recently that my eyesight is deteriorating further. I was operated on for cataracts in 2021 and 2023 (by a French-Iranian surgeon, Dr Marie Callet, whose parents came to France from Iran shortly after the Ayatollah came to power in 1979) and I no longer need glasses. Now, though, I find it difficult to read the clock beside the TV, which is about five metres away. When I see Dr Honey next, I'll mention this.

Chapter 19

A Court Visit

February brings another court visit, but I find out about it only when a guard shakes me awake around 6 a.m. At the first checkpoint, I am allowed to sit on a chair until my name is called.

Once we are on the minibus, two women prisoners and a female guard get in. One of the women has a baby with her. It turns out that the prisoner I am handcuffed to is the baby's father. I offer to swap places so that he'll be seated on the aisle nearer his wife and baby. The guard unlocks our handcuffs so we can exchange places. I wonder why the couple are in prison.

There is snow on the ground in front of the court. My feet are freezing in my flip-flops.

We ascend to the third floor and it's the same judge. This time the hearing is about the two pieces of pottery they found in my rucksack.

'I hope that you realise that these pieces are nine hundred years old and valuable.'

'That's wonderful,' I reply. Is there a reward?' I explain that, in some countries in Europe, the rule is that the value of an item that goes to the state is split between the owner of the land where it was found and the individual who found it. 'If the items go on display in a museum, I would like it to be known that they were found by me,' I add.

'Do you understand that taking the pieces of pottery is a crime?' the judge asks sternly.

'Well, no,' I say. 'I didn't think so, because I wasn't taking them out of the country.' The judge is not happy with my impertinence.

I return to my seat. I am asked not to cross my legs since this is disrespectful. I uncross my legs. As usual, I am asked to sign a document and, inevitably, I refuse and fold my arms. This time nobody insists that I sign and I am brought down to the same room in the cellar of the court complex. It is bitterly cold, so I just keep shuffling up and down to keep my blood circulating. Nobody is sitting down.

I am not back in the prison until just before lunch, so the hot shower will have to wait until tonight.

I ask to see Dr Honey because I discover that my vitamin D treatment, which I take every three months, is missing from my box of medication. I am brought down to the doctor. I explain the situation and he fills in a slip which he gives to Hassan. We go to the pharmacy window and then into the room where I am usually taken for my morning tablet and evening blood pressure check. It turns out that I am going to get an injection. I explain that, generally, in Western Europe, we swallow medicines. Everyone looks horrified and then they laugh when it's my turn to get the injection in my bum.

20 February. Reswan is taking a shower. His bottle of shower gel is on the wall between the toilet and the shower. I move his bottle to the other end of the wall, out of his reach. He doesn't notice me because he has soap in his eyes. It's very funny to see him trying to find the shower gel. I have ducked out of sight and I can hear him cursing. When he sees me, we have a good laugh about my jape.

I decide to make a set of playing cards. These are banned in Iran, so there's little chance of getting a pack sent in. I use the cardboard from cigarette cartons and black and red pens to fill in the four suits. I used to like to play patience on my phone, before I was in here, so playing with 'real' cards is a change. And of course it attracts the attention of my cellmates; in particular Karim, who has been teaching me backgammon and another game with multiple players, which helps me to learn to count in Persian. For the 'board', my cellmates have drawn out the design on sacking from big bags of rice they get from the shop. We use plastic bottle tops for the counters. I also make a cardboard version of 'Shut the Box', a simple numbers game in which players have to match numbers on tiles to those on the dice. I borrow the dice from the backgammon game. We have a draughts game too, but it's not very popular with my fellow inmates.

Benjamin has been able to get hold of bootlegged CDs, including Pink Floyd's 'Another Brick in the Wall', so every now and then, when nobody is looking at the television, we put on some music. Abdullah and Ibrahim are also fans and like to listen to Pink Floyd. Benjamin, who had become depressed since his false releases, has some French singers whom I like, but they make me think of home.

21 February. A surprise today: security delivers a painting to me. It is from eleven-year-old Abel, Roland's nephew's son, who lives in the Montpellier area. It's full of colour, with men 'flying' from the ground to the sky. The words 'peace' and 'courage', in French, are painted around what looks like the Earth. My cellmates are in awe. They ask me to translate the words. Taj gets out a clear plastic folder to protect the painting and it is stuck up just beside the television so everyone can see it, including the guards when they do the roll call. Taj tells me that the painting has to stay in the cell when I am released. I agree. Abel would be proud.

Benjamin and I are told that we must go with a prison worker to record our details. So we are brought along the big corridor, past the staff restaurant and the empty staff swimming pool (the prison was built in the 1960s, designed, apparently, by a German architect). In a huge office, outside which there's a long queue, clerical staff are sitting behind Dell computers. We are photographed, digitally finger-printed and then asked for details of our 'crime'.

We reply 'hostage'. This throws them, because their system, unsurprisingly, does not have that option. There follows some confused discussion and they end up putting down 'security' or 'political' for our so-called 'crime'. Benjamin asks them what this document is for. We are told, not very convincingly, that it's for a new debit card for all the foreign prisoners. When Benjamin and I return, the five other foreign prisoners in our cell are taken down.

In the afternoon, I am brought to the room where I met our lawyer, Ms Halami. There are two men there. One I recognise as the 'translator' for the judge, the one who had told me that I would die in prison. The other man is introduced to me as my lawyer.

I'm confused. 'But I already have a lawyer: Ms Halami. I don't need or want anyone else.'

'Take a seat,' my 'lawyer' says.

I choose an office chair on casters. When I sit down, the chair collapses, and I hit the base of my spine on the stone floor. I am in terrible pain and yell at the two idiots who are staring at me as I lie on the ground. They find me another chair.

When order has been restored, one of them speaks. 'The Islamic Revolutionary Court will not recognise Ms Halami, so you have been given another lawyer.'

I cross my arms. 'I don't recognise this man as my lawyer. I want to go back to my cell.'

'Yes, yes,' they say. 'Once you have signed these documents.' They hand me a pile of papers, all written in Persian.

'No,' I shake my head. 'Absolutely not.' When I return to the cell, I ask to see Dr Honey because my back is very sore from the fall and I need a painkiller. When I am brought into Dr Honey's office and tell him about the incident with the chair, he is concerned. He examines me and when he applies pressure at the base of my spine, I cry out in agony. He writes out a prescription for a painkiller.

22 February. Another court visit. However, after the clothes check, I am brought directly to a waiting minibus. I am not put in handcuffs or shackles. My armed guard and I wait a few minutes when who turns up but a smiling Dr Honey and another man, a nurse. I am very confused. What is going on, I wonder.

At the court we arrive by a back entrance and enter the usual courtyard. In the hall, there are lots of men in gold-braided uniforms. We are invited to take the lift to the fourth floor. There, in a large courtroom, is my appointed defence lawyer and a woman translator, who speaks excellent French. She tells me that she learned her French in Nice and in the 16th arrondissement of Paris (the same area as the Iranian embassy!). There are television cameras, spotlights and a lot of people milling around. I am told to sit in front of a stand with a microphone. Dr Honey and the nurse sit just behind me. I recognise the judge's 'translator', who appears to be at the prosecution's table to my left.

The judge enters and we all stand. It is not the same judge I met before. A man in military uniform goes to a stand, picks up what I assume is the Koran and starts to sing something from the book. This lasts a good ten minutes, with a cameraman filming him and his audience in the courtroom. The judge reads out the charges against me, and the translator translates. I am in a daze with the list of things of which I am supposedly guilty, including that I sent photographs to *The Guardian* newspaper. They even say that the train timetable they found in my bag is evidence against me. I just smile and when asked what I have to say, I deny everything. 'My lawyer' then pleads on my behalf, referring to my poor health and my age.

I am invited to sit down again. On either side of me, I find the two men from the time I was in solitary confinement. They are both wearing baseball caps and medical masks and spend their time on their smartphones. I am asked to stand once more. The judge reads out my sentence. I am given three and a half years for supplying information to an enemy state. However, the judge adds that, in view of my ill health and age, he is going to ask for compassionate release. The lawyer looks very happy. I am asked to sign documents but I refuse to do so because they are not in English or French and my chosen lawyer,

Ms Halami, is not here. This does not appear to be a problem; the court officials just shrug.

Dr Honey is beaming and slaps me on the back. This is good news, surely – it sounds so plausible. I am older and in poor health and, as Mr Houey had told me, there is no case against me. The translator comes over to me to explain that my so-called lawyer will come to the prison tomorrow and that she will give him a book for me, in French, on the life of the statesman and novelist André Malraux. I am led away down to the minibus and back to the prison with Dr Honey and the nurse.

25 February. A cell search. When we come up from our morning break, we are not allowed into the cell. Prison workers and guards wearing gloves are going through my cellmates' belongings. Apparently, they do this every now and again to keep the prisoners on their toes. They do not touch my or Benjamin's bunk. Everything is very ordered and calm. They take a few things away in rubbish bags.

I try to call my father and then Caroline but get no answer, but I do get through to Roland. Our conversation is a little emotional. He talks about work on the house in Banyuls. I tell him we are still getting snow showers in Mashhad. I cannot talk directly about the cold because its taboo to mention our conditions, but I am sure Roland understands.

After the call, I am taken next door to the block director's office, where books have been left for me. I'm puzzled because items are usually left in security next door, where I've just been talking to Roland on the phone. Did they want me out of security quickly?

The lawyer does not show up as promised.

I am ploughing through the *Irish Times* Simplex crossword books. It turns out they are from my cousin, Catherine Phelan, who had been in Iran around the time I was arrested. It's great to have something to stimulate the mind. Someone has also sent us a 2023 French almanac, a wonderful gift. For each day of the year, there is a story – anecdotes about things that happened on particular days one hundred years ago. There are even quizzes and crosswords. I look forward to reading an entry every day. It's a link to home. Another book Benjamin and I enjoy was sent by a friend of his, a big volume of humorous quotations categorised under various themes: marriage, food, animals, politics, literature, religion, and so on. There are quotes from people as different as Groucho Marx and Winston Churchill. I often read it while eating by myself. The Iranians appear to find it funny when we read and laugh to ourselves. I think to myself that these two books should be sent systematically to people like us by the authorities in Europe. Anything that will cheer us up is welcome.

Abu Hassan tells me that I remind him of his uncle. I ask why. He says his uncle had hurt his back after falling off a horse and, ever since, he walks lopsidedly, like me. Not a good sign!

Chapter 20

The Verdict of the Revolutionary Court

26 February. Another court visit this morning. I assume it's to hear the final verdict, that my conviction will be quashed and my sentence ended. A smiling Dr Honey is waiting for me in the minibus; no nurse. Again, we go through the back entrance of the court and take the lift to the fourth floor. This time there are no cameras and far fewer people. The lawyer and translator are there and I point out to the lawyer that he did not keep his promise to visit me. He mumbles something, which the translator does not translate. I am told to stand and the judge reads out the sentence. It is six and a half years, not three and a half years with clemency. I am thunderstruck! I can hear Dr Honey behind me groan. The lawyer and translator look at their shoes.

The judge leaves the room and I sit down. Dr Honey also leaves the room. It turns out that he has gone to see the judge to explain that my health is not good and that I should be sent home. But his appeal is fruitless. He returns, shaking his head. He admits that he does not understand what is going on.

We return to the prison in dead silence.

I tell my cellmates what has happened. They are amazed, all except for Benjamin, who says that there is no proper judicial process for our cases, just like there is none for the political prisoners.

27 February. Today, two prisoners are awaiting execution in the cells beside the guards' office. We never know who they are or what they have done. All we see are their flip-flops outside the cell door.

1 March. In our cell, a number of prisoners are growing plants. I think they take cuttings from the plants in the flowerbed in the courtyard. They are usually kept on the top bunks near the windows beside Benjamin and me. Benjamin points to a plant and whispers to me 'cannabis'! I look closer and can't believe my eyes. The plant is small but it's easy to recognise the tell-tale leaves. But where did whoever was growing it get the seeds? (It turns out that the seed mixture used to feed the birds in the aviary on the floor below contains cannabis seeds.) I am flabbergasted. What a risk these guys are taking. I just do not understand. I am not sure who else knows, if anyone. About a week later, the plant in our cell has disappeared.

This afternoon, there is a bust-up between Yellow Vest and Taj. Insults are exchanged but I don't know exactly why. The two almost come to blows but we and the other cellmates keep them apart. Benjamin and I are holding Taj. I have never seen anyone so angry; it's not easy to restrain him. A guard and prison workers turn up and take the two away. With the help of cameras, they should be able to work out who started the altercation.

155

Taj and Yellow Vest both come back this evening. Taj explains to us that Yellow Vest, who, like Taj, has been in prison for over seven years, was complaining about the space Taj had in the cell. Yellow Vest then started to insult Taj's family and, in particular, his father. They are both in a foul mood. There is little sympathy for Yellow Vest, who is becoming more isolated because of his behaviour. He had a run-in with Abu Hassan a while back. The latter no longer speaks to Yellow Vest and if there is group meal with Yellow Vest present, Abu Hassan eats by himself. Yellow Vest has also alienated me with his talk of Hitler and 'French' players in the football squad.

My blood pressure is sky high when it's checked. Again, I get shouted at for refusing to take their tablet, but I'm determined not to, as long as I'm in here.

As we sit around talking this evening, Taj tells me that a while before I arrived in prison, the block director had him and five others taken down to the courtyard. Three, including Taj, were sent back to their cells. The other three were executed the next morning. Taj is hoping to have his death sentence quashed by the court.

Benjamin comes back from his call to his family looking miserable. He has just heard that his grandmother died a few days ago. The poor fellow tells me that when he cried on the phone, the man in security told him that men should not cry. He is still on hunger strike, his only 'food' coffee with milk and water with a teaspoon of tomato purée in it.

My father was 97 last November. His health is fine but he's a little frail and unsteady on his feet. The idea that I might never see him alive again haunts me. I wonder if my family would tell me if something was up with my father. Would I be able to withstand the shock? I don't know.

3 March. More snow showers. Still cold in the cell. My blood pressure has been high for two days before returning to the 'normal' level. I recognised another prisoner in the medical centre yesterday evening. He's on hunger strike and could barely walk. His eyes were sunken into his head. His crime, for which he received a twenty-year sentence, was converting from being a Shia Muslim to being a Sunni. I helped him back up the stairs to his cell, which was just across the corridor from ours.

5 March. Things are looking up this morning – we're getting new carpets. The three well-worn ones are replaced by new cotton and synthetic ones. I got into trouble a while back because I put a hot pot down on the carpet near the door and it made a big burn mark.

A huge amount of dust is created by this change of carpets, so we end up getting out the vacuum cleaner. The Dog, we discover, is hoarding food under his bed. This makes everyone angry because it brings in cockroaches, mice and even rats. I only saw the cockroaches. It's the same with the fridge: The Dog hoards food there, too, until it's practically crawling out of the tin or plastic box. It's disgusting.

He's not the only one who is careless about how the fridge is used. Some of my cellmates take the warm prison food and put it straight into the fridge, so it never gets really cold. The plastic door of the small freezer compartment at the top is broken, so it flips open every time someone opens the fridge. As a result, food tends to go off fairly quickly.

I talk to Taj about it and he points out that The Dog should normally manage that, as the cell manager. I tell him I know that, but I have never seen it cleaned since I arrived. So we ask our cellmates if we can put in place a monthly rota for cleaning the fridge. Most agree, and we decide to do it the next day, giving time for everyone to get organised. Those cellmates with frozen food can ask the shop next door to store it until we are finished. Part of my plan is to get certain cellmates to throw out 'old' food, thus freeing up space for the rest of us. I mark the containers and bags of my food with the letters 'IRL'.

The next morning, after the first 45-minute break (we are shut in our cells twenty-one and a half hours out of every twenty-four), everyone takes out his stuff and then the strongest cellmates manhandle the old fridge into the washing area, where it defrosts. Then, hot water is taken from the tea urn, and Reswan, The Dog (surprisingly) and Taj proceed to give it a good clean. I try to persuade them to put up a rota but, for some reason, there's not a lot of enthusiasm.

Unlike some areas, the aviary gets cleaned fairly often. There's a door with a padlock to get in. One evening, when a prison worker was cleaning in there, I quietly closed the padlock, without locking it, so that the worker could not get out. I went around to the front to watch his reaction. You should have seen his face. When he turned around, he could see me grinning and then he burst out laughing. Now when someone's in the aviary, and I am around, they take the padlock with them.

8 March. Strange things have been happening in the medical block today. Men in suits came to 'look' at me. I

158

had never seen them before. This evening, the hatch opens and the prison worker manager is there with another man. I can hear them mentioning my name and notice them pointing to me.

9 March. Taj says that his wife saw my cousin, Patricia Phelan, crying on television at a press conference in Dublin. It just shows how many people in Iran watch opposition television and the importance of social media. The Iranian state is trying to control the internet in Iran by controlling access to websites and by cutting access to the web from time to time, but news still gets through.

There are marital/conjugal visits for prisoners. The Dog is the biggest beneficiary in our cell. You always know when he's due to spend a few hours in a bedroom with his second wife because that morning he spends ages in the shower and puts on a clean shirt. Taj's wife brings clean bedclothes when she comes.

11 March. Another French consular visit. The ambassador, Nicolas Roche, says he has a surprise for us. Shortly afterwards, a French doctor arrives along with Dr Honey. The doctor arrived from Paris via Dubai. The French government secured a visa the previous Friday (the Iranian weekend) for this doctor, who works at the Ministry of Foreign Affairs. According to Nicolas, this is very unusual and the Iranians are suddenly extremely cooperative. The doctor examines both of us and talks with Benjamin about his hunger strike. Dr Honey disappears to get something. He returns with our files. The French doctor goes to photograph the results with his phone, but a man from security says no. I hear later that apart from North Korea,

Iran is the only other country that does not share the medical information of prisoners. Dr Honey explains the results and the French doctor takes notes. He tells Nicolas Roche and Dr Honey that Benjamin and I must be hospitalised immediately. Dr Honey agrees.

The next morning, Benjamin and I are brought down to security. Amazingly, there are all the books and presents brought by the French team the day before. Later that day, I am thrilled to talk to Roland. He's in Banyuls. We talk about the painting of some of the rooms that Geneviève, Dany and other friends from Toulouse have done, accompanied by Geneviève's dog Lulu, a Welsh terrier, who has adopted Roland.

The following morning there is no reply from Justin Ryan, but I have the German embassy number on my card. The lady who answers the phone says that Justin is out at meetings. She tells me that her father has heard that my father is old and, apparently, he regularly asks his daughter for news about me. She then starts to apologise for what is happening to me. I ask her to stop.

I am taken to see Dr Honey. My blood pressure has been high for a number of days. He tries to convince me to take some of his medication. I concede. He takes my blood pressure; it's very high. I accept the tablet and place it under my tongue. We wait for a minute or so and when he takes my blood pressure again, sure enough, it's down. So I tell him that he now knows how to get it down, but because this will allow the authorities to say that I am fine, I shall not take these tablets again.

That evening there's a big meal of kebabs and rice delivered from the staff restaurant to everyone. Nobody is too sure why we merit this largesse, but sometimes other prisoners – for example to celebrate the birth of a child – will offer a restaurant meal to all the prisoners in the block. In fact, it's possible to order food from the staff restaurant to eat, but this would not look good in front of my cellmates. I did once order pizzas for a group of us. They were pretty disgusting – barely warm – but it made a change from the mediocre prison food.

While we eat, Benjamin goes downstairs to his workshop.

Chapter 21

Persian New Year and Ramadan

20 March. Tonight the Iranians will celebrate Nowruz, the Persian New Year. We move from 1401 to 1402. It's not the same as the lunar calendar in other Muslim countries, where it's now 1444. The country seems to close down a little, just like in Europe between Christmas and the New Year, with people taking holidays to visit family. Beside the aviary, a table is laid out with the symbols that are found in every Iranian home at this time: plastic coins symbolising wealth and prosperity, decorated eggs for fertility and new beginnings, a mirror to symbolise reflection and self-reflection, and a bowl with real goldfish in it, which symbolise life and the flow of time. (There's a funny part in Jafar Panahi's film *Taxi Tehran* where the filmmaker-turned-taxi-driver picks up two women who are bringing their fish in their bowl to dispose of them in the park, after Nowruz. When he brakes sharply, the fish slide out of the bowl.)

On this occasion, most of the prison workers, as well as some of the guards, wear black long-sleeved shirts. There are two types of religious holiday in Iran: sad ones and happy ones. On the 'sad' ones, the black shirts are also worn. I do not know how many of these holidays there are in Iran, but there seem to be more state holidays than in Western Europe.

Prisoners, especially the prison workers, like to 'show off' how religious they are. Hassan, who sometimes brings me to the medical centre, even has a key ring with a picture of Ayatollah Khomeini on it attached to his belt, so that everyone can see it. I learn that many prisoners who do not practise outside suddenly become very pious in prison. Part of this is to score 'good' points with the authorities. When being considered for parole, the prisoner's conduct, including his religious behaviour, is taken into account. The same applies when a prisoner wants to move to a 'better' block or to another prison.

This year, Ramadan starts on Wednesday, 22 March. This means that Muslims do not eat, drink or smoke during the daytime. So all the cooking times are thrown up in the air and meals become more complicated. Benjamin and I can eat when we want to (of course, he is still on hunger strike) but we cannot cook. Sometimes the kitchens are open only at 2 a.m., so our cellmates have their meals in the middle of the night. Even with the effective sleeping tablets, I no longer sleep well at night. However, my cellmates sleep a lot during the day, so it's a little easier for me to doze in the afternoon.

One evening, there is a lot of shouting and screaming downstairs. It transpires that two prison workers tried to beat up one of the older political prisoners. Apparently, they persuaded him to come to the gate leading into the yard, which is one of the few areas in our block without CCTV. They roughed him up a fair bit before another prisoner came to his aid. The rumour is that someone, probably in the government, wanted to scare the older prisoner. He is not afraid of speaking his mind, including on the phone. As a result, he is not allowed to use any of the three phones in the block but must make his calls from the block director's office. It just shows us that we are not one hundred per cent safe.

27 March. This morning we are told to protect our food and belongings because this afternoon the cell will be sprayed with a chemical to eliminate cockroaches. We are told that we can put our things in the corridor. We all rush to put our fresh food, clothes and bed linen outside, we open all the windows that we can open, then Hussein comes in, with a sprayer strapped to his back. He has no mask. As he starts, we all leave and hang around the corridor. The chemical smell is terrible. This type of event is great for reorganising things, so for the rest of the afternoon there's plenty of activity, keeping my mind from dwelling on life back home.

I see the odd cockroach in our block, but most are dead, scattered around the bins in the courtyard. Is the food that bad?

28 March. I am called down and brought into the block director's office. Dr Honey and another man are there. Dr Honey explains that this 'doctor' has been sent from Tehran to check me medically. The man has a cardboard box from which he removes the equipment to take my blood pressure. The way he handles it makes me wonder if he's really a doctor. He proceeds to take my blood pressure. I have to insist that he give me the reading, which is too high, as usual. He tells me that he will be back again soon.

Today, Benjamin's hunger strike is nearing its 60th day. I can see that his cheekbones are more pronounced but it's in his fingers where I notice the loss of weight; his knuckles are more prominent. He tells me he's finding it increasingly difficult to sleep. I am reading a book called *Why We Sleep* by Matthew Walker, a fascinating piece of work, sent by my cousin Patricia in Scotland. The author explains how there are two brain cycles at play. One is telling our body, 'I am tired. I must sleep,' and the other is saying, 'Do not sleep. Search for food.' So I tell Benjamin that I will sneak him a bar of chocolate later. It works and he has a good night's rest. From then on, I regularly smuggle him chocolate bars. He slips the empty packaging into the crates of food he keeps under his bed and I discreetly get rid of it, making sure the cameras and The Dog see nothing.

Walker also describes how the brain 'protects' us in difficult circumstances. It seems to 'delete' bad memories. I have no nightmares while in prison. In fact, I dream very little.

Two days later, I am brought again to the block director's office. Dr Honey is there with another man, who actually looks like a doctor. He, too, takes my blood pressure and tells me that he has been sent by the Iranian minister of justice and will be back every week. It's the last time I see him.

This afternoon, amazingly, we get a table and four chairs. I know that Nicolas Roche has been working on this behind the scenes because of my back. It's the first time in over six months that I can eat my food sitting at a table. My cellmates are dumbfounded because, as far as they know, this has never happened in the prison. At first, the table is placed near Benjamin's and my bunks, but we move it to the wall below the television. We insist that everyone should use the table, which they do.

One morning, a new prisoner arrives; a very young man from a remote part of north-west Pakistan, near the Afghan and Iranian borders. His name is Achram and he does not even speak very good Urdu, but Taj and Reswan immediately put him at ease. We are told that he's twenty, but we all think he's no more than seventeen or eighteen. In other words, he should not be in our block. He has a wonderful smile. Taj takes him under his wing. Achram has never seen a television. In his village, there is no electricity or running water. As far as we can understand, he is in prison because he and two Iranians tried to assassinate a mullah, a local religious leader. If that's true, the outlook for Achram is not good.

I get a phone call from Justin, who tells me that he has got permission for a consular visit on 5 April. I am delighted. I tell him to bring me a pencil, paper and a rubber.

Chapter 22

A Letter to My Father

2 April. I am not well. I start to get very hot, sweat starts to appear on my brow and I get unsteady on my feet and have to sit down. It's called 'dumping syndrome', caused by a vagotomy operation for ulcers carried out a long time ago and something that is no longer practised because of the side-effects. The immediate solution is to drink a sugary drink, such as Coke or Sprite. I am able to get a drink from a cellmate. When I was younger, I would get over these attacks quite quickly and would be okay a few hours later. But as I get older, they seem to take a lot out of me and I feel exhausted for the rest of the day when they occur. In the evening, I buy small bottles of Coke and put them in the fridge, just in case. My blood pressure reading is high.

4 April. Justin reads me a letter that the President of Ireland, Michael D. Higgins, has sent to my father. He talks about how he and his wife, Sabina, pray for me every evening. The president tells my father that if he needs anything, not to hesitate to contact him directly. I ask Justin to bring a copy of the letter and a Persian translation, so that prison security can see it.

Benjamin is amazed that someone can receive a letter from the president. I try to explain how Ireland, a small country, is very different from France. We tend to be on first-name terms with everyone, even the president or a minister.

That evening, there's a report on the regional news programme on the television. A man in Mashhad has been arrested for murdering his father and then eating the father's heart. Are we going to have a new cellmate in Satan's block? Talking of murder, one of the prison workers, who's a bit dim, is here because he murdered his parents, brother and sister with a knife. I have no idea how long his sentence is.

When I am called to meet Justin Ryan, I tell Benjamin that I am sure that the Iranian with him will be a woman. He does not think the Irish would send a woman to a male prison. Well, sure enough, Justin is with an Iranian colleague with her scarf pulled back, showing her blonde hair.

Justin gives me a big hug and his Iranian colleague politely shakes my hand. Justin is loaded down with books and clothes. It's a pity we are not allowed to be given food. I would love to be able to make a good coffee and drink a cup of Barry's tea.

Justin shows me a letter from the Minister of Foreign Affairs, Micheál Martin. With a pencil, he marks a sentence where the minister writes about my husband, Roland. Justin asks me if, back home, our relationship can be talked about. I say 'absolutely'; I don't want to hide my homosexuality. It's my second weapon, apart from my poor health, to get me out of here. The idea that a European gay man is in an Iranian prison will make for a lot of palaver back home.

Justin and his colleague flew up from Tehran the day before. Flying within Iran can be complicated for diplomats because they are not allowed to use particular airlines and, even then, they may not be allowed to take certain aircraft. A lot of the Iranian airlines are blacklisted by the European Union, as their aircraft and/or management are not up to scratch. For example, in 2009 Caspian Airlines had a crash that killed over 165 people. I took one of their ancient McDonnell Douglas MD-82s between Bandar Abbas, a port on the Strait of Hormuz, and Tehran. I was not reassured to see people still standing in the cabin and phoning friends and relatives as we were heading down the runway!

Justin tells me that he is just back from Brussels. The Iranians have forced the closure of the international German school in Tehran where his children were students, so he's had to move his family to Brussels to find an apartment and school places. While he was away, there was a bit of stress because a replacement, Oisín, coming from Turkey, could not immediately get an Iranian visa, even as a diplomat. So, unexpectedly, I was without my Irish link for a few days. It was so agreeable to hear another Irish accent. Oisín was followed by Sonya McGuinness. I didn't realise, when she was taking down my messages, that she was the Irish ambassador to Iran, based in Ankara.

When our time is up, we return to the hallway, and I hand over all the books, socks, scarves and letters to the security people. Justin's Iranian colleague becomes really angry with the man from security, complaining that it's taking too long for me to get things through security. The other Iranians in the hallway look at their feet as this little woman tears into their colleague.

Later that day, I am taken to the medical centre for another blood test. Nobody tells me why. At around 6 p.m., I am handed a striped uniform and told that I am going for a medical examination. Everyone is very surprised. So I head off in my uniform. But after the clothes check, instead of being directed to the big room next to the courtyard where we wait for the minibuses, I am taken to another room nearby with a chair and a radiator. Benjamin told me about this place. There are pairs of hooks set high up along two walls with dirty white webbing. The floor is spotless, but the walls have dark brown stains on them. This is where prisoners are flogged. The stains on the wall are dried blood. I never thought I would see a place like this in my life. It is horrible. I have heard that some prisoners who are to be flogged hold a copy of the Koran in the hope that the flogging will be less severe.

After a while, I am handcuffed and shackles are put on my feet. I board a bus with two young guards and an officer. One of the guards, as usual, has a machine gun. We head off into Mashhad's evening traffic. It is dark but seeing lit-up shops and all the activity of a busy city makes me feel good. At an attractive square we pull up outside a modern building with shops. We get out and I discover we are going to an ophthalmologist.

We climb the three flights of stairs because the lift is too small to accommodate us all. We enter a packed waiting room, where everyone is staring at me. I sit beside the guard with the machine gun. The officer goes to reception and hands out cash to pay for the consultation. An old lady in traditional black clothes starts complaining to the guard beside me. He ends up taking off my handcuffs. The lady and I smile. I am made to jump the queue. I try to protest, pointing to all the people who are waiting, but the officer refuses and brings me into the doctor's office.

The doctor speaks good English. The officer sits in the corner playing with his smartphone. The doctor carries out various tests on modern-looking equipment. The 'funny' part is reading the chart. In Europe, the chart would have letters of different sizes; here, it's various symbols. I have to say which way they are turned, to the left or right or to the top or bottom. For some reason, I'm wearing my glasses to do this! I mention this, but the doctor just shrugs. He writes out a report and gives it to the guard. We leave and return to the prison. I find it strange to arrive in the evening. It reminds of my first day here.

6 April. On the phone with Ahmeneh, she asks me to confirm my height – 191 cm – and asks me the colour of Benjamin's eyes. Something's up.

The guards now shut the kitchen outside Ramadan cooking time, which is in the middle of the night. However, one afternoon it is open, so I rush upstairs and get my thermos flask so I can fill it with boiling water. Time up, we have to go back to our cell. I ask the guard to wait a few minutes while the kettle boils. He says 'No'. I have to leave the kitchen now. This is the guard who makes life difficult for all the political prisoners. I insist that I am going to wait for my hot water. He is furious. I refuse to give in and take my time filling the flask. I am certain that if I were Iranian, I would not have got away with doing what I did.

8 April. Another medical visit, again around 6 p.m. In the city centre, the minibus stops outside a clinic. This time

I have no shackles, just handcuffs and the blue striped uniform. The officer and guard accompany me in the lift. I discover that we are visiting a cardiologist. The waiting room is packed. The officer has a credit card to pay for the consultation. While waiting our turn, the officer sitting beside me shows me his smartphone. There is a picture of me on some social media site. He smiles, puts away his phone and takes off my handcuffs.

When it is my turn, we enter the doctor's room. He speaks good English. He examines me, then sends me to another room, where I am put on a fixed bicycle and hooked up to electrodes. I have to pedal like mad in the stress test. Then it's into another room for an ultrasound, carried out by a woman. The prison guard is always present. We return to the doctor, who gives the report to the guard. Downstairs, as I stand with the officer who has sent the other guard to find the minibus, a man walks up to me. He shakes my hand and asks me, in excellent English, why I am in prison. I explain my story. The guard beside me says nothing. The man wishes me well and walks away. We return to the prison through the busy evening traffic.

The next day is Easter Sunday and I am able to phone home. I call my sister, Caroline, and she answers immediately. It's fantastic because she's with all her family and Roland in their garden in Sèvres, just outside Paris. Emilie and Craig, close friends of mine, are there too. It was Craig who was accused by my interrogators in October of being a CIA employee! It's brilliant to be able to talk to everyone. They are eating Easter eggs. I miss my annual feast of Cadbury's Creme Eggs. These phone calls are weird: because the line is so good, I get the impression that the person at the other end is in a room next door, instead of thousands of kilometres to the west.

On the Tuesday morning, there is a further medical outing. I am getting to know everyone at the various prison control points. The officer, instead of the usual 'Inshallah' ('God willing' in Persian) says, 'Good luck' as I board the minibus. I now carry my handcuffs and shackles. This time we are going to a university hospital.

It's a huge complex. I have two different consultations. The first is in a room with two doctors and about ten medical students. I am asked questions about my HIV status. One of the doctors examines me. I wonder what the students must be thinking when they see an armed guard in the corner. In another part of the hospital, we wait for ages in a corridor. Everyone is staring at me. I wish I had brought a book to read. When it's my turn, I discover that I am to have an ultrasound of my abdomen. The doctor silently carries out the procedure, writes up a report and gives it to the guard. We return to the prison. I am not sure what all this is about. I suspect that they are checking if what the specialists in France have written in the medical report is true. Or are they checking that I am in good health before they send me home? I think of Ahmeneh's questions about my height and the colour of Benjamin's eyes.

The next morning, I have another hospital visit. This time, the exam consists of a doctor prodding me with an electrode that passes a small electric current through my limbs, which makes my muscles twitch. He dictates to his assistant and says nothing to me. We go back to the prison.

The next day, I am taken to see Dr Honey. He says the results of the tests so far are good. I tell him I am concerned about my deteriorating eyesight. Reading a book with small type in the evening is becoming a problem.

Something is definitely going on. On Saturday 15 April, I am taken to the room in the medical centre where blood tests are taken. However, this time there are two men there whom I have never seen before. They take blood samples, using a tourniquet. The samples are put into a yellow bag that appears to be insulated for ease of transportation.

On Monday, 17 April, there's yet another hospital outing. This time it's an MRI scan for my back. I am starting to get to know the layout of this university hospital. After we go out to the car park, one guard is sent to find the minibus. The officer and I sit on the kerb in the shade of a tree. He takes out his phone and, with the help of Google Translate, tells me that the tree is a mulberry tree and that the fruit is edible. The other guard, with the machine gun still strapped to his back, starts to jump up and pull down branches to pick the small white berries. I get up and help him. I am not sure what the people must think, seeing a prisoner and a guard with a machine gun jumping up and down plucking berries from a tree!

In the minibus on the way back to the prison, the guard reads my medical report and whistles. I ask him what's up. He turns to me and in basic English asks me if I walked from Ireland to Mashhad originally. I ask him why. He says the report on my back is terrible. I am worried because I suspect there's been a problem since the incident in the prison with the broken chair.

Back in the prison that afternoon, I am taken for another blood test, this time by the usual doctor. He injects something into my shoulder and marks it with a pen. He explains that it's a TB test and that I am not to wash for three days. There is no follow-up on the test. However, the next day, on my way to the medical centre, I meet Dr Honey. He takes me aside and explains that the report on my back is worrying and that they will have to operate soon. I am dumbfounded. I tell him I am more concerned about my eyesight. He insists that no, my back is in a bad state and it cannot wait.

That afternoon, on the phone, I explain the situation to the Irish and French diplomats. They are shocked. The idea of me having an operation on my back in any circumstances is risky. Having it done in Iran, with the post-operative time spent in prison on a bed with no mattress, is unimaginable.

Benjamin has just completed 75 days of his hunger strike. He is very frail, but his 'diet' of coffee with milk, my smuggled chocolate bars and tomato purée in hot water is just about keeping him going.

20 April. On television this evening, they show a huge forest fire blazing in the south of France near our house. Iranian television loves showing negative things going on in the West, whether the very violent demonstrations in Paris against President Macron's pension reform, or bad accidents. Indeed, anything that paints a sombre picture of life in the West.

Recently, the other prisoners asked us about the time Macron was slapped by a member of the public when on walkabout in June 2021. Was the criminal executed or did he get life imprisonment? They would not believe Benjamin and me when we said that the guy had probably received only a short prison sentence at most. In fact, he got 18 months, with 14 suspended.

My cellmates' comments about this incident give me an idea. In the front of the almanac we were sent a while back is an official photograph of the French president Emmanuel Macron in black and white. I decide to have a bit of fun. I carefully remove the page from the book. I draw two red devil's horns on Macron's head. I put the page in a plastic transparent folder and stick it to the fridge door where everyone, including the guards, can see it.

Benjamin smiles, but my other cellmates are horrified.

Now, when the fridge gets its monthly defrosting and cleaning, the picture is carefully removed and put back each time. Beside Macron's portrait, another cellmate has stuck up a small colour picture of General Soleimani, the Iranian officer killed in an American drone attack in Baghdad in January 2020. He was, and remains, very popular among Iranians.

21 April. It's the end of Ramadan, at last. Everyone's cooking like mad, and the shop has cakes they've been able to get from outside. It's great to return to normal hours, even if it means that it becomes impossible to doze in the afternoon because of the television.

This evening, a new arrival comes to the cell, a man Taj knows because he has a haulage company and Taj has used his services. We are told that he is now the cell manager, or 'grass' (he reports to the prison authorities what goes on in the cell), replacing The Dog. He explains that he has been condemned to death and has been offered this job, which none of the Iranians in our cell wants, in the hope of getting his sentence commuted to life.

The Dog is staying but won't be in charge any longer. A while back, most of us had signed a letter asking for a change of cell manager, because The Dog was so useless. This man is tall, in his late fifties. He is pale and appears to be ill. At the start he sleeps on the floor in a corner, despite there being free bunks. He also speaks Urdu, so is able to talk with Reswan and Achram. He makes little attempt to interact with Benjamin or me; I'm not sure why.

I have read 47 books since my imprisonment.

23 April. This morning and again this afternoon, Benjamin and I are unable to get through to the French embassy. We call our lawyer, Ms Halami, but she's none the wiser, nor is Justin. When we get through to the French on Monday, we learn that this is not the first time their phone lines have been cut. Christian, the consul, tells me that sometimes they have to send their Iranian personnel home because there are demonstrations in front of the embassy with the participants bussed in for the occasion.

The following evening we watch *Mary Poppins* on television. Benjamin tells me that this is the Iranian edited version and to watch it closely. You remember how the film starts – Mary coming down from the sky with her umbrella? Well, that's been cut. Only Allah comes to earth from the sky. The part where Mary sings with the chimney sweeps has also been deleted. In fact, most of the parts where she sings have been cut, because women are not permitted to sing in public. So the film lasts only about 45 minutes.

There are a host of rules governing male and female interaction in Iran. Men are not permitted to touch another woman who is not their mother, their wife, or their sister. I saw a television series once where a woman has a heart attack while a plumber is working in the house. This man, in a panic, has to go and find help because he is not allowed to touch the distressed woman. If a woman falls in the street, the film is cut at that point, and we see her walking again because it's impossible to show what probably really happened: a male pedestrian helping the woman to her feet. If there are clips from foreign television channels on a news broadcast and if the female presenter has a plunging neckline, everything below her chin is blurred. Prisoners are not allowed to have in their possession photos of their wives, mothers or adult daughters. The same goes for alcohol, which is strictly forbidden. When there's a scene in a bar, for example in a western, the bottles behind the bar are all blurred.

We hear from our lawyer, Ms Halami, that she will be back in Mashhad on Tuesday 25 April for a court appearance for Benjamin's case and she will also try to visit the Revolutionary Court on my account. There will be another French consular visit on Thursday, so it's a busy week.

My leather work with Benjamin is moving along well. I have made a leather handbag for my sister: Caroline's husband, Pierre-Fréderic, works for Hermès, the luxury fashion house, so that should be funny. I have also made two shoulder bags for Roland and myself in camel skin. Reswan, to supplement his income, and now Achram, are both churning out the stuff. There are beautiful chess boards and wallets. Benjamin is fed up with all the negotiating with the prison workers to get the leather and to sell what has been made by the prisoners. The prison workers who sell the work try to screw us, so Benjamin decides to stop and use up what's left of the leather. He suggests making a big overnight bag. My stitching is not brilliant – I do not have enough patience – so we arrange for Achram to do the stitching and I pay him, half now and the rest when the bag is finished. He's delighted; at last he has some money.

Achram, like Reswan and Taj, is very religious and spends a lot of time praying, kneeling on a prayer mat and rocking while he chants in a very low voice. Taj and I are trying to teach Achram English and he's learning fast. Just like the leather work. He wants to learn. I got some books from Justin, the Irish chargé d'affaires, including *The Old Man and the Sea,* which Iranians know well and is easy. I also got a copy of *Animal Farm* for Dr Honey.

Some books that get through security surprise me. For example, Antoine de Saint-Exupéry's book *Lettre à un Otage* (*Letter to a Hostage*). If the title had been in English, I do not think it would have been delivered. I think prison security were not bothered translating the title. I was later to learn that I was also sent a copy, in English, of *The Count of Monte Cristo*, another tale of imprisonment. I never got it.

After Benjamin's court appearance, he returns, looking confused. Nobody appears to understand what's going on. There had been a suggestion that he might be offered parole, but who would pay the bail was the question. There was confusion about whether he would have to stay in Mashhad or could be moved to the French embassy in Tehran. Now, it transpires that parole was not on offer.

At the consular visit the next morning, the French team look glum. Nicolas Roche, the ambassador, tells us that he has been naive regarding the judicial system in Iran.

He pleads with us not to make any fuss and to tell our families the same. Benjamin and I explain that we are at the end of our tether and that we cannot take much more of this.

Benjamin tells Roche that he will not leave without his van. All his savings are tied up in the bond for his van and unless he somehow gets it back to France, he will lose the bond. We've discussed this a lot, with me trying to persuade him that it is more important to get home as we are, rather than trying to persuade the French to include the van in any negotiations. But to no avail. I remember Benjamin even saying once that he would be willing to stay in jail for a few more months, if it meant that he could get his van home, too. Imagine my reaction. I tried to convince him that the French government would help in this exceptional situation.

The ambassador tells me that there is likely to be an Irish consular visit in a few days. The Irish ambassador to Iran, Sonya McGuinness, based in Ankara, will come. A cousin has sent me a message saying that she is going to protest to the Irish that there should be no talk of opening an embassy in Tehran while I am still incarcerated. I knew the Irish would use this as a bargaining chip in any negotiations.

Chapter 23

The Trouble with the Bookmarks

27 April. I have been making leather bookmarks for a while. Benjamin gave me one when I arrived with the word 'Azadi', which means 'Freedom' in Persian, stitched into it. Taj helped, improving the script to make the stitching of the word clearer, and I was churning them out, much to the amusement of the prison workers. In Benjamin's workshop, I cut out the pieces of leather and punched the holes. The stitching of each bookmark I would do back in the cell.

This evening, a guard and two prison workers come into our cell. This guard is the nasty piece of work with whom I had a run-in over hot water. He insulted Taj once in front of everyone during a roll call. He appears to spend his day reading the Koran.

'Please,' he says crisply. 'Give me the bookmarks.'

'Why?' we both ask.

'It's not allowed,' is his answer.

'But Benjamin has been making them for ages, long before I came,' I protest. There is silence in the cell; all the other prisoners are watching. The guard has a face like thunder. 'Maybe we can stitch another word onto them,' I suggest. 'Like "prison" or "Mashhad".'

He is not happy. He asks Benjamin to follow him and the prison worker. 'Don't give him the bookmarks,' Benjamin says. It is all very tense. I am sure if we were Iranian, the guard would hit us. After about twenty minutes, Benjamin returns with just the prison worker. 'We'll have to hand over the bag,' he says. 'If we push it, there'll be more trouble and it's not worth it.'

Chapter 24

The Irish Ambassador's Visit

1 May. This morning I am called down early for Sonya McGuinness's visit. I am taken to the meeting room by a big friendly guard whom I have encountered a few times before. When we arrive in the room, the ambassador rushes up and hugs me. It is wonderful – I become tearful. The guard in the corner cannot believe his eyes. It's forbidden for men and women who are not family to behave like this in public. On top of which, Sonya's hair-style would raise eyebrows even back in Europe. It's a little punkish. Also, her scarf is slipping back, showing most of her hair, which is also against the law in Iran.

We sit down and I tell her that I'm fed up staying quiet and that I can't take much more of my incarceration. I say that I'm willing to hold on until 15 May, after which I will start making trouble. She replies that she fully under-stands.

I ask her if she could do a favour for me regarding another prisoner. Could she let his embassy in Ankara know that he is here in Mashhad prison? I've written down various pieces of information on my arm, so I turn my back to the guard in the corner and roll up my sleeve so that Sonya can copy down the information.

When my time is up, the ambassador and her assistant hand over lots of things, including books, but above all, a copy of the letter written to my father by the President of Ireland, with a translation into Persian. As usual, security impound everything. Let's hope they do not take a week to check it all.

When I get back to the cell, Taj tells me that Achram has been taken away, he thinks for more questioning. I am worried.

3 May. Today Ahmeneh reads me two messages over the phone, in English, from the pupils of a French school, where a long-lost friend, Cathy Harris, is an English teacher. The Paul Émile Victor College is in the town of Branne, situated about 35 kilometres east of Bordeaux. The letters are from children who are 10–11 years old.

Dear Bernard,

Your story has touched us all.

We send you our support and we hope that you are still healthy. You seem to be a strong man, so please stay strong until the day you are released!

We do hope that you will be released soon; in the meantime, may God help you.

Will you come to meet us in Branne?

We are thinking about you, we are now many who know about your situation. Everything will be fine, Bernard, we send you all our positive thoughts.

6ème A, Collège Paul Emile Victor, 33420 Branne

Amandine, Chloé, Dounia, Léonie, Raluca, Camille, Mayline, Elise, Enzo, Noa, Ethan, Maélie, Rafaël,

Evan, Naïa, Mathis, Emma, Sam, Clément, Sarah, Ludmilla, Odin, Eliot, Zoé, Yanis, Alyssia, Nina.

The second one reads:

Dear Bernard,

We hope that you are fine.
   Life in prison must be difficult.
   Are your cellmates nice to you? How do you keep busy?
   We are all aware of your situation and we offer you our moral support and also, defend your freedom.
   We would like to send you drawings but we were told we cannot!
   We hope that you will be released soon and we send you all the courage you need.
   6ième E class, Collège Paul Emile Victor, 33420 Branne
   Louna, Emy, Evissa, Ludivine, Théo, Julian, Mayana, Noa, Maeva, Sheymae, Alan, Margot, Lola, Tara, Gaspard, Jules, Warren, Teddy, Margaux, Noémie, Sharon, Gabriel, Alicia, Mathis, Waël.

Later, I will learn that my father also wrote me long letters during my imprisonment, which I never saw.

Now, about two days after her visit, I finally get everything that Sonya McGuinness brought, including the letter from President Higgins. Let's hope the Iranian authorities are paying attention to the mounting interest in my case in Ireland. I just cannot bear to envisage myself spending another month in this prison, and the idea of six and a half years' imprisonment is just impossible to contemplate.

After that long, my father will not be alive when I get out, I'm sure. He'll be 98 this November (2023). My separation from Roland is also becoming harder and harder. On each phone call he sounds close, but he's in the free world.

If there is no visible progress by 15 May, then I might attempt to commit suicide. The problem is that the prison authorities have recently removed anything sharp from our cell. I wonder if this is a coincidence, or if they are putting two and two together about my mental state. I have to find a solution.

What I have in mind is to cut my wrists in the shower after the last roll call of the day. Really, I do not want to kill myself, but just to do enough harm to scare everyone, here in the prison, as well as the Irish and French authorities back in Europe. I know I'd be taking a huge risk, but I'm already doing so by not taking the medication for my blood pressure or heart condition.

5 May. I've found a solution, out in the yard. The raised flowerbed in the courtyard has some broken tiles on it. Discreetly, I am able to break off a sharp piece of tile and bring it up to our cell. The next problem is hiding it. Then I have an idea. In the two searches conducted in our cell the guards have never bothered to examine the food. So where better to hide the piece of tile than in the fridge, in my open tin of tomato sauce?

Part Three
Freedom

Chapter 25

The Final Days

The week that followed those dark thoughts seemed like an age. The broken piece of tile remained in my tomato sauce tin as I contemplated my fate a while longer. Then, on Thursday 11 May, everything changed.

It was around midday when the cell door slid open and Hassan asked Benjamin and me to come downstairs to security. As usual, we weren't told why. I wondered if something needed to be explained to me, which Benjamin would translate.

There were no other prisoners in the corridors, but what struck me as very strange was that the three 'public' phones along the wall were no longer there! Was it because one of these recently installed phones was giving trouble? Why would they take them all away? Why were there no prisoners in the kitchen? With a rota system in place for the cells in our block, there were always other prisoners using the kitchen or just chatting. And at this time of day the courtyard was usually open.

Hassan took us into Mr Djadahi's office; he was the director of security. Usually there were at least one or two security men there, but Djadahi was alone behind his desk. He asked us to sit down and then announced that we were to be freed today. Benjamin put a steadying hand on my knee. Neither of us could quite believe this was happening.

We were told that we would have to write a document, in French or English, stating that neither of us would pursue legal action against the state of Iran or the prison for being badly treated. Without speaking to each other, Benjamin and I both said we would not write such a document.

Mr Djadahi told us to return to our cells. Hassan, waiting outside, looked grim. He brought us back upstairs in complete silence. Usually, he would chat to Benjamin and crack a joke about my attempt to say a few words in Persian, but now he said nothing.

Back in the cell, everyone wanted to know what had happened. They sensed that something was up. Benjamin said that he thought our release had been fully organised, and that the Iranians could not reverse the decision.

About twenty minutes later, the cell door opened and Hassan and another prison worker came in and told Benjamin and me to pick up our gear. There was cheering and smiles all round. It was about 1.30 p.m. I had sorted my books into two bags: the first was a prison bag of the books that had personal inscriptions and that I wanted to keep. Then there was a bag of other books that I would leave behind in the cell. There were hugs and handshakes with Taj, Karim, Reswan, Essan and the three Bahrainis. We did not shake hands with the other three prisoners: The Dog, Yellow Vest and the new 'grass'. I was able to slip Taj my prison credit card. I had given him the PIN code a while back. The money left on it was to pay for Reswan's phone calls to his family in Pakistan and for the balance for the leather work done by the other Pakistani, Achram, if he ever came back from interrogation.

Benjamin was ready with his boxes of leather work tools and equipment, in addition to his prison bag of books. I could take away nothing with my handwriting on it. I had destroyed my notes over time, so there was only one month of notes left, which I tore up and put down the toilet. The four of us trooped downstairs to the corridor outside the guards' office.

There was still nobody around: something important was happening today, I concluded. I think the gate to the courtyard was closed so that prisoners out there could not talk to us.

All our belongings were thoroughly searched. Written documents were removed, as well as our prison phone cards. You should have seen their faces when the guards opened Benjamin's boxes! There were plastic jars full of studs and zips! He was taking them back to France. Someone came out of security with a white plastic bag for me. It was full of things that had not passed security. There were the two hot water bottles Ahmeneh had sent from the French Embassy in Tehran, as well as scarves, woollen hats and socks, but no books and no CD of The Chieftains or DVD of Jacques Tati's film *Mon Oncle*, which Roland had sent me. I was to discover much later that Kenny's bookshop in Galway had been sending me books, many of which I never received.

Benjamin went to wash his hands in the kitchen and called out to the men in the yard that we hoped we were on our way home. The news would travel fast through the prison network. We shook hands with one of the decent guards and walked out of 6-1, Satan's block. We proceeded down the long corridor to the main security check. Poor Benjamin, who was almost 100 days into his hunger strike, found it difficult and we had to pause a few times along the way. At the clothes check, there were three or four plainclothes men waiting for us whom I had never seen before, as well as the usual guards; I assumed they were from the security services. Our bags were examined, but when they saw Benjamin's belongings, they gave up. I handed over the receipt I had been given when I first arrived in prison and they had taken my boots and belt. A cloth bag was brought out with a metal tag attached, but it did not contain my possessions. A guard began to search for my belongings. The plainclothes men were getting impatient, so I gave up and walked off in my flip-flops. At the next security check, our photographs were taken beside a clock and then we went on down the corridor towards the main prison exit. But before we reached the main gate, we were directed to two unmarked cars in the yard.

The Peugeot and Kia both looked brand new. Benjamin and I got into the Kia after putting our bags in the boot. The other car contained, I think, four men, one of whom was filming. He was wearing a baseball cap, sunglasses and a Covid mask.

Nobody told us where we were going. Was it to the airport or to a hotel? What we did not know was that the French ambassador, Nicolas Roche, and his colleagues had been outside the main gate since 7.30 a.m. along with two private ambulances. However, instead of leaving by the main gate, we took an internal road behind the prison blocks to exit on the other side of the complex. I think it was the road I had been driven on when I first arrived.

We drove along the Mashhad ring road, which I knew well from 'outings' to the Revolutionary Court and also to the clinics and hospitals. The other car was beside us, with the man still filming. Benjamin, sitting on my right, kept his clenched fist up so that the camera could not avoid it. After about twenty minutes, we left the dual carriageway, drove down a residential street and pulled up outside an unmarked building. I began to think we were going to be rearrested or that we had been taken to another interrogation centre. I was really stressed and sweating with fear.

One of the men pressed an intercom in the wall and we were buzzed into a small room. We all got out of the Kia and trooped in, the cameraman still recording it all.

We were guided to a room with seats and low tables around the walls. The tables had teacups and I think foil-wrapped biscuits on them, just like the room for the consular visits at the prison. The two men in suits who were there introduced themselves and said that they were from the Iranian foreign ministry. One told us that the French diplomats would be along shortly and offered us tea. We both refused. After what I'd been through, I couldn't contemplate accepting their hospitality.

Benjamin and I sat opposite them while the man with the camera sat in a corner, I think still filming. Benjamin kept holding his clenched fist up to the camera. The foreign ministry men exchanged some words, nodding towards us. I asked Benjamin what they had said. He told me that they were going to rearrest him! I don't think they were joking.

Nicolas Roche, Christian Furceri and another Frenchman arrived. We were each asked to sign a document in Persian.

We were reluctant but Nicolas whispered that the document was worthless because we were signing it under duress, and it was not even on headed notepaper. We both signed and the ambassador put his signature on some other documents. The third French diplomat was apparently able to read Persian. The consul was sent to get the two private ambulances that Nicolas told us were going to take us to a hospital for a complete check-up and that we would be flying home the next day, Friday 12 May. I was excited, but terrified at the same time. I wanted this nightmare to end, but at the same time, I was very worried that something would happen at the last minute. I remembered Benjamin's devastation at his false release earlier in the year.

The ambulances turned up a few minutes later. With a male nurse in each ambulance, we were driven to the hospital. We were put in wheelchairs, brought to the top floor and installed in two luxury rooms. The director of the hospital, a heart specialist, explained that they were going to carry out a battery of tests on us, including X-rays.

I discovered that the en suite bathroom had a European toilet with toilet paper. Heaven. I sat on it for a good twenty minutes and used metres of toilet paper. I'd had over seven months of squat toilets and just a hose to clean up.

An X-ray machine and equipment for an electrocardiogram were wheeled into my room, followed by a nurse, who would be taking blood tests. While the doctor was with Benjamin, Nicolas Roche came in. He explained that the plane that would fly us out was staying overnight in Tbilisi, the capital of Georgia, and that we should take off from Mashhad airport around midday, if all went well. I asked him if Benjamin had mentioned the remark made

194

by the foreign ministry men about rearresting him. He had not. Nicolas was visibly shocked.

The doctor's wife then came in for a chat. A charming woman, dressed in a flowing green dress, she was, it turned out, a professional pianist. It was fantastic to talk face to face with a woman after being isolated with only men for so long. Up to now I had spoken to women only over the phone, apart from meetings, in the prison, with my lawyer, Ms Halami, and with the Irish ambassador, Sonya McGuinness. The doctor's wife explained that it was complicated for her and her daughter to accompany her husband abroad to medical conferences, because the Iranian authorities were obviously concerned that they might not return. She showed me a clip on her Instagram account on her mobile where she was singing at home, while her daughter played the piano. She explained how the police called her in for an explanation and told her to remove the clip. Women are not allowed to sing in Iran.

Next came Laurent, the third French embassy official. It turned out that he was from the DGSE (Direction Générale de la Securité Extérieure), the French overseas secret service organisation. He had a folder under his arm with a list of questions for me. They mainly covered the events leading up to my arrest, the solitary confinement and the interrogation sessions. Laurent asked me to describe the people concerned. On his phone, he had a version of Google Maps with better aerial views of the prison complex than I had seen before. Laurent then showed me a picture of the shrine complex and I was able to identify the pedestrian square where Mike and I had been stopped and the street where the prayer room used for the interrogation was located. I was able to give Laurent the approximate travel time from the prayer room to the first interrogation centre and the time it took to drive from the first centre to the second one.

Laurent then focused on our block within the prison. This was not too difficult because block 6-1 was not far from the staff swimming pool. I was able to pinpoint the medical centre and the holding pen where we would wait to be taken by minibus to the court or elsewhere.

Nicolas Roche came back to explain that the doctor was going to sleep in the room next to ours, just in case. The rest of the team were staying in a nearby hotel and would see us the following morning.

Benjamin was exhausted but was sitting up in bed with a big grin on his face. His hunger strike was over. Dinner was served, with a knife and fork – the first, for me, in over seven months. In prison, we had eaten with a spoon only.

There was a television in my room, but I did not put it on because of the bad memory of having it blaring in the cell for twelve hours each day. There was a beautiful box of tea bags and '3 in 1' coffee mixes (coffee, milk and sugar in a small packet). The selection of teas included a cumin-flavoured tea, which was really excellent.

The door to our rooms had a frosted yellow window and I kept looking through it to see if someone was passing by outside. Later, I got up to walk along the corridor. Benjamin was fast asleep. A screen had been placed in the middle of the corridor, so nobody else could see into our part of the corridor and our rooms. The doctor, in a crumpled shirt, came out to check that I was okay. I am not sure if it was the worry that the Iranians would turn up to take Benjamin or both of us away, or perhaps the excitement of impending freedom, but I found it impossible to sleep.

Chapter 26

Leaving Iran

Friday 12 May. I sat in my room, drank more tea and waited for the French diplomats to turn up. After breakfast, Nicolas Roche came to our rooms and confirmed that the plane would arrive in Mashhad around midday. We went downstairs and met Ms Halami and the rest of the French team. There were lots of hugs and she called her colleague back in Tehran, who had been involved in our cases, so we could speak to him. Then Nicolas Roche said he had a surprise for us. It was a video call with Ahmeneh, my guardian angel at the French embassy for the last 222 days. It was Friday, the beginning of the Iranian weekend, but there she was on the screen: the face behind thousands of dictated and read words. It was great to see her at last. Tears of emotion rolled down my face.

Nicolas gave each of us a *laissez passer* document, which would allow us to enter France. The photo on mine, I was to discover, was from the website that Caroline had set up. It was dated 20 April 2023, which, we would later learn, was around the first attempt to set us free. At the time, I can remember Ahmeneh asking what I thought was a curious question about the colour of Benjamin's eyes. Only now did I understand why.

Christian Furceri, the consul's, principal interest was in the type of aircraft we were going to take. Nicolas sent him to check out the ambulances that were to transport us to the airport. The ambassador was on his two phones almost continually, telling us of the progress of the plane from Georgia. Then suddenly, he swore. The Iranian ambassador in Dublin, Dr Eslami, had sent out a tweet announcing our release. Now, all the press would be aware of something the French were very keen to keep under wraps.

We were wheeled out to the two ambulances and then set off for the airport. On the drive, my Iranian nurse shared some biscuits with me. He told me about his life taking patients from the city of Mashhad to different parts of Iran. His English was good. Religion came up when he asked me how I'd managed to cope in prison. He could not fathom the idea that I was an atheist. I tried to explain that if there was a God, I would not have been in prison.

When we arrived at Mashhad International Airport, we were not allowed to enter the airport compound. Nicolas Roche went off to see what the problem was and returned to tell us that the authorities would not let us in for another half an hour, so we waited, roasting, in our ambulances. The sun was intensely hot. Fortunately, the diplomats brought us water. Nicolas said he was not sure if there were going to be cameras, so we should appear as weak as possible when getting out of the ambulances and sitting in our wheelchairs. It wouldn't do if the authorities saw us skipping to the plane in good health.

We were wheeled into the VIP lounge of Mashhad International Airport. It was absolute luxury; European frequent-flyer lounges do not compare. There were flowers, big couches, thick Persian carpets, cakes, beverages, even a fridge of Iranian caviar for sale. A few well-dressed passengers were waiting there. I am not sure what they thought of our little group.

The man from the Iranian foreign ministry was there too. He asked us if the ambassador was going to buy us caviar! He took away our *laissez passer* documents to be stamped. We were now free to leave Iran.

We declined the caviar and waited in our wheelchairs. Nicolas told us that the plane, a Falcon 900, had landed and would soon be ready to take off again. I was sad not to have met the people in the French embassy in Tehran who had looked after us from a distance, who had shared our worries and concerns and who had been the intermediaries between home and prison.

Then we saw a woman and a man walking towards us along the corridor leading from the tarmac. They had come off the plane. The woman was from the French foreign ministry, and the man was a French doctor, David Tran-Van. They were here to take us home. We said our goodbyes to Nicolas and the rest of the embassy team, and our wheelchairs were turned towards the security check. The jet was right up beside the door that led to the tarmac. We walked up the steps of the plane, to be greeted by three pilots and a nurse, Alexandre Arnaud. They immediately put us into two beds. The plane started to move off as soon as the door was closed.

One of the pilots came into the cabin. 'How long will it take to get out of Iranian air space?' I asked him. I was very worried that a last-minute attempt by some Iranian faction, obsessed with their internal power struggle, would try to stop us, blocking the plane on the tarmac. I had vivid memories of the Ryanair plane flying between Athens and Vilnius in May 2021, which was forced to land in Minsk, the capital of Belarus. They had even used a MiG jet to escort the Irish Boeing 737. A journalist opposed to the Belarus regime, Roman Protasevich, and his girl-friend, Sofia Sapega, were taken off the aircraft. He was later sentenced to eight years in prison.

'It's okay. We're flying north towards the border with Turkmenistan and it'll only take about twenty-eight minutes,' he reassured me.

The jet took off. Lying on the bed, I could see the dry landscape passing below. I started to cry, thinking of all the people I was leaving behind: Taj in prison, Mike and his family, as well as lots of friends I would probably never see again. Was Mike still in prison? I had no idea.[1] It was a very difficult moment. I tried to focus on home, but it was impossible. I cried silently.

The doctor and nurse carried out a battery of tests. They were very proud of their equipment, being able to measure your blood pressure and heart rate at the same time. And to top it all, we were given real coffee. Pure bliss.

Suddenly, the pilot came back to the cabin to tell us we had left Iranian airspace. There were howls of joy, laughter and tears. Soon we were allowed to get up and sit in the jet's leather armchairs. I visited the toilet, where the taps looked as if they were made of gold, but, strangely, they did not work!

The pilot explained that the jet's baggage hold had been converted into a fuel reserve. With the extra fuel, the aircraft was capable of an incredible range.

---

[1] I would later learn that Mike had been released after a couple of days' questioning in October 2022.

I was talking to the lady from the French Ministry of Foreign Affairs and told her that I had planned to commit suicide on 15 May, using the piece of tile to cut my wrists, and that I had not been taking the medication for my blood pressure from the beginning of my imprisonment. She looked shocked but said she understood.

After flying north for a while, we turned west and crossed the Caspian Sea, where I had swum almost eight months before; we flew over Azerbaijan and weaved around troubled Armenia to reach northern Turkey. Then we headed north-west for Paris. I persuaded Benjamin to ask the captain if he could sit in the cockpit since this would probably be his only opportunity to do so. He did and he stayed there until not long before we were due to land. I relaxed in the cabin, drinking more of the excellent coffee.

All through the flight, I found out later, the lady from the French foreign ministry was in constant contact with Paris. About an hour before we landed, she came and told us that there was a sizeable press contingent waiting for us at Le Bourget airport, but she assured us that the authorities would keep them at a distance.

Benjamin asked the doctor how long it would be before he could eat a tartiflette, a cheese and bacon dish from the French Alps. The reply was 'in about fifteen days'. A huge smile spread across Benjamin's face.

For the final approach, I replaced Benjamin in the cockpit and chatted with the pilots. Le Bourget, just a few kilometres south of Charles de Gaulle airport, was Paris's first airport, opened in 1914. It is now used for business traffic, as well as for visiting heads of state.

As we taxied to the terminal building, the pilot explained that instead of stopping in front of the building, he had been asked to put the nose of the jet into a hangar. On getting closer, we could see armed police on the roof of the hangar and scattered around the entrance. I asked the pilot if some important head of state was arriving at the same time. He said no: all this was for us. I was astonished. When the plane's nose was in and the pilot had cut the engines, we were towed further into the hangar. The pilot could not believe his eyes. They were getting the whole jet into the sparkling white hangar and closing the doors behind us.

The pilot and I stood up, and he went to open the door beside me. He put down the steps and, with a smile, said to me, 'There's a message for you.' At the bottom of the steps was a mat with 'Welcome' written on it in English.

I walked down the steps and then heard Roland's voice shouting, 'My Bernard!' There he was, striding towards me, arms outstretched, with Caroline beside him. I could see a big crowd behind them and a photographer. There were hugs and kisses; I squeezed Roland in my arms, then hugged Caroline, who was smiling broadly. She held up her phone, so I could see and talk with my father back in Dublin, where his carer, Mihaela, was connected via smartphone.

I turned around to see where Benjamin was. He was walking slowly behind me. I went over and put my arm around him as he walked towards his family. I was able to meet his parents and his sister, Blandine. She had been battling for his release for over three years.

As we made our way across the hangar, people came towards us. The first group were French officials from the Ministry of Foreign Affairs. Stéphane Romatet, the director of the Crisis Centre, was there with the two of his staff who had been most involved with Roland and Caroline on a daily basis: Ms Françoise Puig-Inza and Ms Claudine Remm. Again, lots of hugs and smiles. Next came the Irish diplomats: Maurice Cotter from the Irish embassy to France and Dónal Cronin from the Department of Foreign Affairs in Dublin. They had a message for me from Micheál Martin.

Another French gentleman introduced himself as M. Emmanuel Puisais-Jauvin, the *chef de cabinet* of the French minister of foreign affairs, Catherine Colonna. Roland had been in touch with him previously, trying to get to speak to the minister directly, but without success.

We were directed out of the hangar and into two ambulances. Police motorcyclists were waiting, too. After saying goodbye to everyone, I set off in my ambulance for the military hospital, Bégin, on the eastern edge of Paris, along with the nurse from the plane and Roland. The motorcade was preceded and followed by vans of police and motorbike outriders blaring through Friday evening's traffic. Benjamin and his sister, as well as the doctor, were in the other ambulance.

It took us a very short time to reach the hospital. A medical team was waiting for us. The plane's medical team handed over their reports and bade us farewell. It was a touching moment, leaving these two men, who had been such an important part of getting us out of Iran. Roland also left, promising to be back the next day.

Benjamin and I were taken in wheelchairs into lifts and along corridors to two rooms, which turned out to be as far from the entrance as you could get. It transpired that the press, who had been unable to see us at the airport, had turned up that evening at Bégin hospital, but they were told that we were at the 'other', more famous, military hospital in Paris, Val-de-Grâce, so they all headed there. But Val-de-Grâce has been closed since 2016!

In the room was a large travel bag with clothes from the French foreign ministry: tracksuit bottoms, underwear, sweatshirts. Benjamin and I shared them, as a stream of medical personnel came in and out of our large rooms. Our first French meal was served, but there was no wine. I was able to have a long shower and get into a comfortable bed without having to worry, for the first time in months, about what was going to happen the next day.

I knew, however, that I was going to need something to help me sleep. Having had sleeping tablets in prison every night, it was not going to be easy to resist them now. I told the doctor that I would need something strong. As usual, I was not believed, and sure enough, I had to call the nurse before long to give me more sleeping pills. Eventually, with the blinds down, in pitch darkness and almost total silence for the first time in months, at around three o'clock in the morning, I was able to fall asleep at last.

Chapter 27

Beginning My Recovery

Bégin Military Hospital is located in Saint Mandé, on the eastern edge of Paris. It was established in 1858 for the victims of the war in Crimea, a strange coincidence because there were Ukrainian soldiers there when we arrived, receiving treatment.

The next morning, despite it being a Saturday, the hospital started to run tests on Benjamin and me. They even brought in their eye specialist because I was very concerned about my deteriorating eyesight. It turned out that I had glaucoma and would have to start treatment at once.

Back in my bedroom, overlooking the hospital grounds, an army officer was waiting for me. She explained that Caroline and Roland could visit me whenever they liked. For other friends, I would have to give their details so that the authorities could check them. Only when I gave the green light could they visit me. She warned me that there were journalists ringing in, pretending to be family and looking for information about our health, so I had to be careful if I met a stranger in the grounds. She gave me a card that would allow me to move freely around the hospital.

I looked in on Benjamin next door; he was still asleep.

Roland arrived with a big smile and croissants. We went downstairs to get coffee and then walked outside and sat in the sun. I took off my prison flip-flops and walked barefoot in the grass. It felt wonderful. Then it was just the two of us sitting on a bench under a tree. When Roland and I went back upstairs to my room, a nurse was waiting with a menu for the next two days. We were, after all, in France. What a change! Roland had brought me clothes from home as well as some money. I asked him to buy a cheap mobile for me so that I could talk to my father and other family and friends.

While Roland was out buying a phone, I had a visit from Dr Guillaume, the hospital's head psychiatrist. She was going to look after Benjamin and me, even after our hospitalisation. She asked me to tell her everything from the beginning. The first session lasted for about an hour. It was good to be able to talk to someone about what I had been through, a real sense of relief that someone could understand the emotions and thoughts that were going through my head. I did not want to burden Roland or Caroline because they had had a terrible time too. I was not the only hostage. Caroline, Roland and my father had also been hostages for the previous 222 days.

Dr Guillaume reassured me that I could take all the time I needed. I could stay in hospital as long as I wanted and if things became difficult when I returned to normal life, the hospital would be there for me. When Dr Guillaume left, she met Roland, who was waiting outside my room. She went off with him. I learned that Roland and Caroline had been helped by an organisation called Hostage International, based in the UK. It had been recommended by the Irish Department of Foreign Affairs. They have correspondents around the world. Hostage International had helped Caroline and Roland to find suitable psychiatrists and had given them advice, including information to help them manage my return. Roland brought me one of their documents, which had been written to help returning hostages. They assigned me a Frenchman, Adrien, to advise me about returning to my previous world. I was able to call him to discuss, for example, how to go about getting the administrative side of things sorted. Before talking to the media, I also spoke to Georgina, an expert in the Hostage International organisation. She advised me on how I could deal with invasive questioning and explained that I didn't need to accept every interview request I got.

Then it was down into the bowels of the hospital for X-rays of my back. The staff were very understanding and took their time with me. Unfortunately, there were problems at the base of my spine.

A good French lunch was followed by a nap. I was able to call my father and tell him that Roland and I would be flying to Dublin to see him as soon as possible. After lunch, Caroline came to see me. It was an emotional meeting because she had been on the front line right from the beginning. She had participated in dozens of interviews on Irish, French, UK and US media. Later, I would see scores of articles and radio and television interviews, but today I still find it very difficult to read or watch them. I discovered that my cousin Mary, in New Zealand, had organised all the books that had been sent to me. She had arranged it through Kenny's bookshop in Galway. I was amazed at what had been done by so many people on my behalf. I also spoke to Alisdair, my cousin Patricia's son, the documentary television producer based in Scotland. He had come to Dublin to make a short film of my father and Caroline talking about me. When I saw it for the first time, I cried. Alisdair filled me in on some of the other media actions he was involved in.

The next day, a Sunday, I woke up around six o'clock. Breakfast was a long way off, so I got dressed and went outside. I decided to go to a café just opposite the hospital gates. By the time I had walked there, I was exhausted. I could not believe that I was so weak. I suppose it was not surprising because, for over seven months, I had had almost no physical exercise. It would take time to get my leg muscles back to their pre- imprisonment level. To think that I used to take part in ten- and twenty-kilometre runs in the Pyrenees! I missed being out in the mountains near Banyuls so much.

Roland had told me not to eat the hospital lunch, because he had a surprise. He had been to our local market, where a number of the stall-holders knew about my situation, and he turned up with a selection of hams, pâtés and other pork delicacies. It was the food I had missed the most during my imprisonment. I would have liked a glass of wine but that would have to wait.

Chapter 28

My First Night at Home

After a few days, Roland suggested that we eat lunch in a restaurant across from the hospital. I asked him to bring a cap and sunglasses because I did not want to be recognised. I was given permission but told to be careful. The place seemed so busy and crowded. At the traffic lights, I was afraid to stand at the edge of the footpath. I moved away from the other people around me. The restaurant had a dish of the day – pork in mustard sauce – which was what I ordered and ate with relish. With my cap and glasses off, I got a few stares but that was all.

During the following days, I continued my journey back into society. I was taken to the hospital gym, where a physiotherapist put me on a bike and made me walk on a treadmill. It was very tiring: I could cycle or walk only for about fifteen minutes. After three days, I was given permission to spend a night with Roland at home. I was so happy. I was going to see my home for the first time in eight months. Roland got out a bottle of champagne that had been sitting in the fridge since October 2023, when a good friend, Sylvie from Perpignan, had brought it, thinking it would lift Roland's spirits. He told her he would open it when I was released. When we opened the bottle that May evening, the cork shot off and half the contents spewed out – a celebration!

Roland had prepared a great meal and there was red wine at last. There was also cheese and then cakes from a local pastry shop. We went to bed early. It felt so good to be beside Roland after such a long and harrowing experience. I slept well and didn't dream. In fact, I never have had any nightmares about the prison itself, but I now suffer from violent nightmares that wake me at night.

The next morning Roland wanted to accompany me back to the hospital. I declined because it was on a direct metro line from our flat. I'd manage, I assured him. Roland went to work for the first time since I'd been incarcerated. At that point, the day hospital, where he worked as a psychologist looking after adolescents, had immediately told him to stop and put him on paid leave, which later became sick leave. Now he was able to return to normal.

The metro back to the hospital broke down, so everyone had to get out and find another means of transport. I took a packed bus, standing room only. The bus in turn had to deviate from its usual route due to roadworks. I started to panic. I got off the bus and phoned friends to help me find my way to the hospital. I still did not have a smartphone – a friend, Nicolas, was organising that – so I had no online map. I was not actually far from the military hospital, but I was lost. Roland's phone was off and Caroline's was too. After a few minutes I got Agnes, who was able to guide me to the hospital. I arrived in a state. When would I be able to get about independently, I wondered.

However, the military hospital gave me permission to go to Banyuls with Roland for a week. They locked my room during my absence, an amazing service for a hospital. To get away to see nature was really of great benefit to me. I had been surrounded by walls for so long. To hear birds singing and just to sit outside in silence with Roland and a glass of wine was paradise. I could see the sun rise over the Mediterranean from our bed. I was almost at peace with myself in our house in Banyuls. I could see all the work Roland's friends from Toulouse had done. How they had painted my office, as well as the living room. On the grounds around the house, scrub and dead trees had been chopped for firewood. I was able to meet friends and have some great evenings that week. It did me a power of good.

Chapter 29

Meeting the French Minister

One evening not long after I returned, the French Foreign Ministry invited Roland and me to come to a debriefing session. Nicolas Roche, back from Tehran, would be present, as well as members of the crisis team, and Benjamin and his sister Blandine. I was expecting us to be asked for our views on how everything had been handled, what our recommendations were, what the ministry could have done better, and so on. But the session really was just a polite conversation.

Still, Benjamin and I pointed out how difficult it was to get the administrative side of things organised. There was no 'one-stop shop' where we could get everything done, rather than having to deal with each administration separately. But it was emotional to see Nicolas again: there were hugs all round.

During the meeting, the door opened and in walked Catherine Colonna, the foreign minister. 'I heard you were in the building and wanted to say hello.' She came round the table, shaking hands. There was no emotion in her face. Her staff had just done a brilliant logistical job of getting us out of Iran and she had hardly anything to say. Roland and I were flabbergasted. The next morning, the minister appeared on Europe 1 radio station and talked about Benjamin and me. She explained that we were still extremely tired after our imprisonment in 'Ukraine'. The journalist corrected her.

My first media interview was with Lara Marlowe, the *Irish Times* Paris correspondent, who came to our flat. Lara had covered the French side of my situation from the start. Roland and a good friend, Luce Dulucq, had organised a concert at the Irish Cultural Institute in Paris and Lara had given it extensive coverage in the *Irish Times*. This new article came out on 29 May in a two-page spread, with pictures of Roland and me, smiling. My father was very proud of the coverage.

I was also contacted by the famous war reporter, Florence Aubenas, who writes for *Le Monde* and has written a number of books of investigative journalism. She wanted to interview me. Florence had been taken hostage in Iraq in 2005. She had been kept in a cellar in Baghdad for 157 days in terrible conditions, so she knew something of what I'd been through.

She arrived at our apartment in Paris on Sunday 4 June with her photographer and a bottle of champagne. We talked for four hours, sometimes comparing notes on our recovery and what the first days of freedom were like for us both. She was amazed that no member of the government had been at Le Bourget airport to welcome us back. She explained that the then French president, Jacques Chirac, had been in regular contact with her family. He was also at Le Bourget when Florence got back to France. I told her that Benjamin and I, while in the military hospital, were very surprised not to get a call from the French president, Emmanuel Macron, or the prime minister, Élisabeth Borne.

Florence's article appeared in *Le Monde* on 17 June 2023. A full page with a colour photograph. The article was brilliant. Florence was able to get across the injustice of the scandalous hostage 'industry' operated by the Iranians.

I have difficulty even now reading the articles written about me while I was in prison. I start to read, but I have to stop. It's too difficult. I can feel the emotion welling up inside me. The same goes for the television and the coverage, for example, of the vigil at the Iranian embassy in Dublin.

I am amazed by what other people were doing for me. People I never met before, people I have not seen in years. How could they all put so much effort into fighting for my release? I ask myself all the time how I can thank them.

Chapter 30

Rebuilding My Life

In admin terms, getting my old life up and running again wasn't without its issues. I contacted American Express to block my old card and order a new one. The lady at the other end of the phone, when I explained the situation, was very patient and understanding. She asked me if I had declared the loss of all my things to the police because my travel insurance might cover it. So the next day Roland and I went our local police station. When they heard my story they were very helpful. Roland had declared me a missing person in October 2022, so now that file could be closed.

I spent over two hours with the police officer detailing the circumstances of my arrest in Iran and listing everything that had been taken from me. With the police document, American Express bent a number of rules and paid money to cover some of what had been taken from me. They had, after all, provided me with repatriation insurance. This is obligatory in order to obtain an Iranian visa, and the American Express document clearly stated the dates of my stay in Iran.

Maurice Cotter, from the Irish embassy, had told me to apply for a new Irish passport online, and then send him the reference to expedite it. I received the Irish passport about ten days later. However, with the French administration, it was to take a lot longer. I did not apply for a new French passport but just for a new identity card and driver's licence. The French Ministry of Foreign Affairs had given me a letter requesting that my case be treated quickly. It was not too difficult to get the appointment, but it then took weeks before I received the documents.

Both Benjamin and I were surprised that there was no designated group or agency to help people like us. We later found out that there's a fund to help people in our position, to which we were denied access. But with the help of a lawyer, who took a percentage from our gains, we got access to some funds.

Everyone I met working in the different agencies was very understanding and surprised that I was not given priority.

A few days later I met my doctor, Pauline Campa, at St Antoine Hospital. She had done amazing work, sending to Iran two long detailed reports on my health and the risk I was facing as a result of my imprisonment. These were translated into Persian by the French embassy and passed on to the Iranian authorities. The same was done by my eye specialist, Dr Marie Callet at Foch Hospital on the outskirts of Paris. My rheumatologist in Paris, Dr Mickael Rose, had also sent a report about my back and problems I had with my knees: sitting on the floor and sleeping in a bed without a mattress would be terrible for my back.

One evening, Roland told me that while I was in prison he had received a call from Nicolas Théry at the Crédit

Mutuel. I was flabbergasted. I was a member of the supervisory board of my local branch of the Crédit Mutuel, which is a larger version of Ireland's Credit Union movement, a voluntary unpaid position. Nicolas is the CEO of Crédit Mutuel – CIC, one of Europe's biggest banking groups. He had explained to Roland that if there was something to be paid for my release, the bank would help.

The branch manager, Marie-Rita, was able to help Roland with my bank accounts, both personal and professional. Other members of the board got very involved. Joelle and Pierre took part in a demonstration for the Iranian hostages on 28 January 2023 in Paris, at which even Nicolas Roche, the French ambassador, was present.

I went to meet Nicolas Théry in person at the CIC head office in Strasbourg in Alsace in mid-May 2024. I got a very warm welcome from Nicolas and the president of the group, Daniel Baal. Nicolas explained to me that he was friends with Hélène Tréheux-Duchêne, the French ambassador to the United Kingdom. She, in turn, knew Nicolas Roche. Nicolas Théry contacted Roche in Tehran to see how the bank could help. Nicolas also wrote to the French minister of foreign affairs, Catherine Colonna. Everyone was telling him to stay discreet and not to rock the boat. I explained that that was exactly the wrong tactic. All ex-hostages I spoke to agreed that their cases must be to the forefront of the media. Staying quiet is what the Iranians want.

We also discussed the cause of Cécile Kohler, who is from Alsace. She was arrested along with her partner, Jacques Paris, in May 2022 and imprisoned in Evin Prison. The bank, through their ownership of a number of regional papers, has been active in promoting her cause. I told

Nicolas that I felt that things needed to be brought up to speed, like having a big banner on the façade of Strasbourg City Hall with a counter indicating the number of days she has been held. Big gestures like this would really aid her case, I felt.

Chapter 31

Home

On 8 June, Roland and I flew to Dublin to see my father. Dónal Cronin of the Department of Foreign Affairs had arranged a discreet entry into the country. I had been contacted by the Irish media and had said I would be available to meet them once I had been able to thank the Irish government.

At border control at Charles de Gaulle airport in Paris, I handed in my Irish passport, but I was stopped. The policeman asked me if I had a 'problem' with the police. I said no but that there might be information on my case on file. This was to become a regular routine, each time I passed through French border control. Once, as I was coming back from London, it took over half an hour for me to get through French immigration control. Everyone was very apologetic, but it made travelling even more tedious. It was Adrien of Hostage International who, using his contacts, was able to find the right person to get me removed from the list that came up each time my identity was checked.

My father was expecting me. It was really emotional. He proudly showed me all the press cuttings that were spread out on the dining table. But he was most proud of the long letter sent him by President Michael D. Higgins. He read it out with so much feeling. Physically he appeared in good form, but I was to discover that he had become confused over the past few months and had difficulty trying to work out where places were. This got worse over time and, in February 2024, he entered a home.

On 20 July, I returned to Dublin with Roland to thank everyone involved with my release. There were to be Irish press and television interviews. My sister Caroline was also coming over from France. On the afternoon of Tuesday 25 July, my father, Caroline, Roland and I went for afternoon tea with Micheál Martin, in Iveagh House on St Stephen's Green. There were various members of the team there who had been involved in my release, including Sonja Hyland, the deputy secretary-general of the department. Sonja had been part of a delegation that was dispatched to Tehran shortly after they became aware of my arrest. In May, she had worked closely with the Irish ambassador, Sonya McGuinness, on accelerating my release. I discovered that the freeze on opening a new Irish embassy in Tehran had upset the regime. Sonja told me that the Iranians had wanted a roadmap for the opening of the embassy. She had replied that there was a roadblock called Bernard which had to be cleared up first.

Micheál Martin explained that he had talked with his opposite number in Tehran, Hossein Amir-Abdollahian, as well as having called in the Iranian ambassador to Ireland to explain the situation to him.

The next morning I had an appointment with the whole team in the department. Over good Irish tea, they asked me what could have been done better or differently. I said that the fact I had Justin's mobile phone number was very reassuring. The system for taking down messages was complicated because Justin had to type out my message as I slowly read it out. If there had only been a system where the Irish diplomat could just record the message and someone back in Dublin would then type it up. Our phone time was very precious. While we were in prison, the French embassy never gave us a mobile phone number for emergencies.

There was a discussion about items I most appreciated getting: books and crosswords, followed by comforts such as warm clothes. Once Justin and I joked about him sending us a potato masher. It would have been very useful, but the security people would probably have seen it as a weapon, like the hot water bottles, and not given it to me.

I also learnt from the team that the letters I had dictated to my father were printed out in a typeface that looked a little like handwriting. And as a further bonus they were printed in green!

Chapter 32

A Year On

It's now May 2024, a year on from my release. What's changed in my life? Everything. I am not the same person. I have a very different perspective on life. Now, I want to enjoy life with my husband Roland and Ulysses, my Irish Labrador. I was always rushing to do so many things. No more procrastination. I want to reduce the stress that used to be part of my everyday life. For example, instead of taking my morning coffee at the counter of my local café, I now sit at a table outside and enjoy watching the world go by. I want to take every opportunity to meet friends and family and to take time out with them.

I break down in tears less often now than I did at the beginning, but I never know what's going to set me off. At an opera recently, *Madame Butterfly*, I cried when the heroine, Cio-Cio-San, realises that she will never see Pinkerton again. It made me think of never seeing Roland again. It's something I thought about a lot when I was in prison. The idea of never seeing him again terrified me.

On one occasion, Roland and I decided to watch what was described as a comedy with Catherine Deneuve. The film, *L'adieu à la nuit*, started off well. Then there was a flashback in one of the characters' minds: scenes of a street in ruins. There was a little boy sitting on some steps crying, a tank heading in his direction. I started to tremble, and the tears rolled down my face. We had to switch off the television.

At dinner with a friend, Geneviève, in Toulouse, one of her guests, Laurent, was dressed in a long-sleeved black shirt. Again, I started to tremble and someone at the table asked me if I was okay because my face had gone white. When I explained, Laurent promised that the next time we met, he would not wear black. It's very strange: if the person was wearing a short-sleeved black shirt or if the sleeves were rolled up, I had no negative reaction.

There are many occasions that have become complicated since my release. I no longer listen to the news each morning as I brush my teeth. On television, violent war scenes, cells or prisons make me leave the room. As a daily buyer of Le Monde, I can no longer read any of the war stories. The summer after my release, in Banyuls-sur-Mer, the mayor asked me to make a short speech at the village festival. The local band struck up the Marseillaise, the French national anthem. Again, I started to cry.

Sleeping is problematic, too. For the first few months after my release, I had some terrible nightmares, with a lot of violence. The sleeping tablets usually get me to sleep, but around 4 a.m. I am wide awake again. Dark thoughts have become less frequent, but there are occasions when I am so much in despair that I feel like putting an end to everything. The military hospital's psychiatric section has twenty-four-hour telephone coverage, so in theory I am never alone. But working up the courage to call the number is another thing. Dr Guillaume has kept me on sick leave. I see her in person, or by video link if I am out of Paris, at least once a week, sometimes more often, depending on what is happening to me. We discuss my nightmares, situations that make me uneasy, like the sight of men wearing long-sleeved black shirts, the formal dress of Iran, my dark thoughts. Over time, things have got better but I never know what might trigger a reaction. I am still uneasy in crowds.

Now, the sight of the Iranian flag chills me, from the fridge magnet of the flag stuck to the fridge when I returned to our apartment in Paris, to the Swedish television studio where I was being interviewed about a Swedish hostage in Iran, when a large flag flashed up on a screen beside me. In Iran, these flags are everywhere and they are not isolated: for example, on a road bridge there could be twenty flags fluttering in the breeze. They are a reminder of my trips to the court, handcuffed, with shackles on my feet, and the armed guards with their pistols and machine guns who accompanied me. I felt terrible and when a technician asked me if I was all right, I explained that I wasn't, and why. A few seconds later, the flag was replaced by a picture of Easter eggs, it being Easter weekend.

I am still on sick leave and it has been recommended by my doctor and by the military psychiatrist who sees me weekly that I do not return to work. I have been diagnosed with post-traumatic stress disorder, which, in a funny way, is reassuring because it puts a label or name on how I feel or react. There's something wrong with me, but now I know what it is.

My back and knees are still giving me trouble, as is my glaucoma. I now also have a slight stoop. A painful stress fracture in my left knee was discovered earlier this month, following an MRI scan. My doctor thinks that the conditions I was kept in, and the prison food, both contributed to this new problem. My hearing has deteriorated and I am seeing a specialist at the military hospital.

Roland and I are both big cinema buffs, sometimes going twice a week to see a film. However, this has become complicated. Even if I choose a 'suitable' film, i.e. one with no violence, or one not set in the Middle East or Central Asia, I cannot predict what I'll see on the trailers that will be shown before the main film. I hardly ever look at the television news and, in the press, I tend to skip any news of war or violence, which sometimes means there's not a lot to read.

Reading books has become complicated too. I used to read a lot, but since I have returned home, I have read only one, *A Bit of a Stretch: The Diaries of a Prisoner* by Chris Atkins, about the documentary maker's stay in Wandsworth prison in England. Benjamin, my fellow prisoner in Mashhad, and I used to talk a lot about what prison is like in Ireland or France and Chris Atkins' account is very interesting. However, the most startling thing is that a prisoner in a democracy knows the length of his/her sentence: in Iran, you never know.

I used to travel a lot, to places as varied as Indonesia, Finland, Paraguay, Algeria, Sao Tomé and Principe, the USA, Zimbabwe, Palestine ... but now I prefer to visit more stable and 'safe' destinations. I shall probably never return to Central Asia unless there is a change of regime in Iran. I hope one day there will be and that I shall be around when it happens. I feel sad when I think of all my Iranian friends. At home, Roland has put all the Iranian bits and pieces we've collected over the years, like Persian carpets and Iranian cookbooks, in a cupboard. I don't know when I shall be able to take them out again.

The French government have at last recognised that Benjamin and I are entitled to financial help, as previous hostages have been. The French government scheme, the FGTI (Fonds de Garantie des victimes des actes de terrorisme et d'autres infractions), which helps victims of terrorism and similar incidents, has been of some help. It is managed by the French insurance companies. All property insurance contracts in France include a fee that goes to this organisation. It can also help the families of hostages. From talking to other people, I'm not sure if there's an equivalent in other European countries. Neither the Irish government nor the European Union have offered any financial assistance.

I now know that Benjamin and I were released in exchange for the Iranian diplomat Asadollah Assadi. He was being held in prison in Belgium, where he had been given a twenty-year sentence for plotting a bomb attack on an Iranian opposition meeting in Paris in 2018. This exchange was code named 'Blackstone'; I think after the 18th-century English judge. The Belgian aid worker Olivier Vandecasteele, was also part of the exchange. Olivier was released shortly after the two of us in late May 2023. We have since become good friends. Olivier is trying to get better recognition by the EU of the hostages and I am travelling to meet with him and EU officials at the European External Action Service (the EU's ministry of foreign affairs) in Brussels later this month.

I have also become very involved in the case of the Swedish hostage Johan Floderus, an EU employee who was arrested in Tehran in April 2022. His family and the Swedish government kept it quiet for the first five hundred days of his incarceration. No doubt they thought they were acting in his best interests, preventing an escalation, but as I have shown throughout the account of my experience, putting pressure on the Iranian government by drawing public attention to hostages is a more effective way to push for their release.

In France, I am working with people in the judiciary, who are trying to put something in place for returning hostages on the administrative front. For example, my pension rights for the period as a hostage were affected: at present there's a 222-day gap in my pension, the period of my imprisonment. For the moment, French social security has refused to acknowledge the nature of my absence from France and to reinstate the pension for the period. I have appealed their decision, so we'll wait and see. In late May, I was also asked to return all the money paid to me during my sick leave. The administrative problems continue.

All these separate pieces of my life, from the admin to the activism, give me a sense of purpose and help me to make use, in some way, of those terrible months in Iran. I have no idea what the future holds, but for the moment I'm focusing on returning not to my old life, because that is gone now, but to a new one. I am not the same person who set out for Iran in September 2023. Physically and mentally, I have changed and my life here in Paris has also changed as a result. But I am still surrounded by those who love me and who fought for my release. My father has lived to see me return from Iran; Roland, while upset and angry at what I've been through, is by my side. I have an immense amount of psychological and emotional support. All this is worth living for.

Appendix

Caroline's Account

Caroline Massé-Phelan

I managed to hide the fact that Bernard had been imprisoned in Iran from our dad for ten days after the date Bernard was due home. I knew that if our dad found out, it would be hugely upsetting for him. He was 97 and had already lost his son, our brother, Declan, to lupus in 2006. I knew that if I told him, it would accentuate his own fear of dying.

And I was right. When I told him, he kept repeating that he wanted to see his son before he himself died, and that burden, in addition to being at the forefront of actions we took towards Bernard's liberation, weighed incredibly heavily on my own state of mind, mental health, and everyday life.

These first ten days were like a ticking clock, as Roland and I were desperately trying to find out more about Bernard's situation and how to get him home before having to tell my father. Roland was in daily contact with the French Ministry of Foreign Affairs, and I was in touch with the Irish Department of Foreign Affairs in Dublin. It was an entirely new ordeal, launching me into an unfamiliar world of diplomacy, national interests and geopolitical matters. The Irish Department of Foreign Affairs, while being very supportive and understanding, told me that, since Bernard had gone to Iran on his French passport, the French would be leading negotiations.

I quickly understood that this went beyond an issue of a person being wrongfully incarcerated. As I learned that other EU citizens were being held unlawfully in Iranian prisons I realised that it was a tiny part of the very complex issue of the Middle Eastern policies of not only France and Ireland, but the EU at large. I was beginning to see that Bernard's imprisonment was not going to be solved quickly, and I could not keep it from my dad any longer. By the tenth day of Bernard's imprisonment he had contacted his local garda station and requested to file Bernard as a missing person. I then had to fill Dad in on the fact that we had learned that Bernard was being held in an Iranian prison in Mashhad.

Little by little, I informed friends and family of Bernard's terrible situation. They were an amazing support and without their help I would not have been able to manage. A group of concerned family and friends developed into a support committee with weekly meetings, agendas, roles and to-do lists. We reached out to everyone we could think of before we went to the press. Hostage Worldwide and Hostage International gave us great advice as well as psychological support.

At Christmas, as Bernard's health and morale declined, we decided to go to the press in Ireland to inform them about Bernard's case. We felt that even if Bernard had travelled to Iran on his French passport, it was better to highlight his being an Irish citizen, given Ireland's less controversial position on the international stage. We hoped that by going to the press, and contacting Irish TDs, there would be more pressure on the Irish and French governments to push the Iranian government to release an innocent man.

Being flung into the media spotlight, juggling my job and all the while receiving daily messages from Bernard about his misery took a toll on my mental health, my sleep and family life. Days revolved around getting Bernard home and looking after our father. When we finally got news of Bernard's imminent release, I didn't believe it. We had lived through other moments during his captivity when our hopes were raised, then dashed, and I didn't dare believe that this would not be another. Seeing him walk off the plane in Paris into the sparkling white aircraft hangar was surreal.

I am so grateful to all those involved in his release for bringing him home. My dad got to hold his son again and friends and family are still celebrating.

The Press Strategy and Vigil for Bernard

Eoghan Corry

As soon as we learned of his incarceration, Bernard's family and friends in both Ireland and France were devising their own strategies to get him home. His sister Caroline was faced with a dilemma. The initial approach was to avoid publicity, so as not to offend or provoke Bernard's captors, in the hope that they would release him without fuss or fanfare. By Christmas 2022, it was clear that this was not achieving results at the required pace.

I am a journalist and as a regular on Irish radio and television, having had a previous career as a political commentator in the Irish press, my advice to the family was to devise a simple three-stage message that could be repeated often, a mantra in every communication:

1. Bernard is an Irish citizen.
2. Ireland has no quarrel with Iran.
3. Bernard was in Iran to help the country and promote Iranian tourism.

This was the basis for the first press release about Bernard's captivity, which went out on 27 December. I also advised that the campaign should be led by Caroline, to avoid any solo runs or social media posts by family members and supporters. The *Irish Times* ran its first story on 3 January, and continued to support the campaign, with the other nationals, the *Irish Independent,* the *Irish Examiner*, and the Dublin editions of English newspapers following in the days afterwards. The main Irish broadcasters, RTÉ television and radio, Virgin Media television and Newstalk radio all highlighted Bernard's plight.

The impact was immediate. The Taoiseach, Leo Varadkar, and the Tánaiste and Minister for Foreign Affairs, Micheál Martin, were both alerted to the situation. Department officials set to work. Ireland was due to reopen an embassy in Tehran, a process delayed by the pandemic, and the family's goal was to make Bernard's release a condition for the reopening.

To their credit, Ireland's politicians showed an immediate willingness to cast diplomatic niceties aside to pursue Bernard's release. When the Irish minister met the Iranian minister at the end of January, Bernard became the main topic of the conversation. The Iranian minister said he was 'personally invested' in the case but that the Iranian judicial system was separate and Bernard's case was in their hands. He also said he was 'committed' to improving Bernard's conditions and getting him calls with family.

On 11 January 2023, some brave Iranian nationals living in Ireland protested at the Iranian embassy and called on the government to expel the Iranian ambassador to Ireland. Many had family at home in Iran and joined protests, at clear risk to themselves and their loved ones.

The media support proved crucial: Conor Gallagher in the *Irish Times*, Edel McAllister, Kate Egan and Joan

O'Sullivan in RTÉ, Ralph Riegel in the *Irish Independent*, Neil Michael in the *Irish Examiner*, Christian McCashin in the *Daily Mail*, Gráinne Ní Aodha in the Press Association, and dozens of others who worked behind the scenes in other newspapers, Newstalk, VMTV and other broadcasters. The French media, led by *Le Croix* and AFP, picked up on the Irish coverage.

A support committee website went live on 12 February. Eventually, 8,000 people signed the petition for Bernard's release. But while there was momentum in Dublin, he was facing a new setback: a summary trial in Iran on 26 February.

The family decided early in March that it was time to intensify the campaign further. They held a press conference on 8 March, hosted by Paul Gallagher, general manager of Buswells Hotel. The venue was no coincidence: Buswells Hotel is opposite the Dáil, the Irish parliament, at Leinster House. The press conference was fronted by Bernard's cousins, Greg O'Corry-Crowe, a scientist, and Patricia Phelan, a barrister. Another cousin had produced a video which featured Bernard's father.

The press conference lasted just under 30 minutes, packed into a small room in the hotel, microphones in a row upon the table. The short video was shown (it was also used to front the report by Joan O'Sullivan on the RTÉ *Six One* news). The questions were functional: about the Iranian legal process; the process of communicating with Bernard through Justin Ryan, an Irish diplomat based in the German embassy in Tehran; prison conditions; and the advice from the Department of Foreign Affairs. Greg told those attending, 'There are many significant dates that could see the release of Bernard. The festival of Nowruz, the Iranian new year, is on 20 March. This is a festival that hails the return of the sun, the spring equinox. We would like to hail the return of an Irish son to his father.'

Patricia Phelan reinforced the message to the media that 'publicity keeps you safe.' She said it was not a moment to normalise relations with Iran. 'The Irish embassy closed in Tehran; to reopen it will be seen in Iran and through the world as Iran getting some sort of seal of approval from Ireland, that relations have improved. Is this the moment to send out that signal, the moment that an Irishman may die in an Iranian prison? An innocent, ill Irishman? It is just not the moment to do it.' When asked if Bernard was a pawn in a wider game. Greg replied, 'The man in the street thinks that.'

The press conference also publicised a vigil that would take place outside the Iranian embassy on 30 March. The choice of language was important. Greg emphasised that this was 'a vigil, not a protest'. For the vigil, family members arrived from the length and breadth of Ireland, as well as the scattered Phelan and Corry diaspora from around the world. They held flowers outside the embassy. Some came with the sign of the feminist movement in Iran: WOMEN, LIFE, FREEDOM. Even at the age of 97, Bernard's father was not too old to join the barricades. His was the photograph that graced the evening news bulletins and the following day's newspapers. Here, Bernard's cousin Kathy Phelan remembers the vigil:

The Vigil
Kathy Phelan

On one side of Mount Merrion Avenue were a hundred relatives and friends, carrying banners and polite messages asking for Bernard's freedom. Cars hooted in support as they slowed down and passed. On the other side, we faced the closed gates and shuttered windows of the deserted Iranian embassy in Dublin.

People had come from all over Ireland, England and France to be there. We were desperate to do something. Bernard had been missing from our lives since October 2022, and we knew he was not well. His sister Caroline had kept us well informed about her efforts with diplomats in France and Ireland, and yet there seemed to be a stony silence in response.

30 March 2023. Under a grey spring sky we brought daffodils and laid them outside the high walls surrounding the building and at the metal gate, in a gesture of friendship and peace. Caroline had been clear that this was a vigil, not a protest. Given the age and frailty of some of the people there, it would have been a wilful misinterpretation to describe it as in any way a demonstration. The gardaí looked on and probably realised that, given the presence of a 102-year-old gentleman (Hugh O'Neill, a long-standing friend of the family), there was unlikely to be any trouble, and their afternoon would be peaceful. Uncle Vincent stood up from his chair and, with Caroline's help, slowly, with dignity, walked across the busy road to deliver a letter asking for his son Bernard's release. As we watched, no one said anything, but they must have wondered if Vincent would ever see Bernard again and felt the poignancy of the fact that he had lost his other son, Declan, in tragic circumstances. Tears welled. Then we waited and the initial uncertainty about how to behave dissipated. People began to connect, realising they were distantly related, second cousins twice removed, or had attended the same party in Bernard and Roland's flat in the centre of Paris, or were connected through a mutual work colleague, or had run a marathon with Bernard, or owned a puppy from the same litter as his dog. The atmosphere became relaxed, and although the sense lurked that our efforts were futile, we made the most of the occasion, even having fun. And then, of course, we walked down the road and found a pub. We were delighted when the television news flashed up on the screens, and there we were. We may have achieved something after all.

A Letter from Myriam Frégonèse (Roland's Boss)

24/03/2024

Dear Bernard,

If it's ok with you, I am going to write you the letter which you never received while you were being held captive. Firstly, because back then, we didn't actually know each other. Also, because in order for it to be written, you had to have been released.

The day I discovered that something was about to happen was just after the October Bank Holiday. Roland, your husband, the man that I have seen every day for the last quarter of a century in the day hospital where we work, calmly sat down opposite me, just the two of us in my office, his face grave. I could feel the sense of worry moving through him, until it overtook him completely. He told me of the sudden silence that had fallen over the past few days, a silence that could have been due to the sometimes unreliable telephone connection, depending on what region of Iran you were visiting for your travel research, or that could mean something more sinister.

He had never spoken about you in such detail. We had always maintained a certain reticence between us about our private lives, notwithstanding the genuine

regard we had for each other. Our professional friend-
ship was of the kind you share with someone with
whom you have worked five days a week over many
years: based around our patients, our workplace, our
colleagues, albeit with plenty of laughs, about pretty
much everything and anything, characterised by
Roland's extraordinarily easy manner. He would just
get on with everything in a calm and serene way
notwithstanding all the noise and the occasional fury
of our workplace.

But now, on this day, I could feel his sense of calm
ebbing away, and see clearly that the person sitting in
front of me was now filled with anguish, and I got the
feeling that my intuition was unfortunately right, that
something very serious was indeed happening.

Not long afterwards, it was confirmed. The words
which would tell us what we already knew. Loss of
liberty, weeks and months of struggle ahead, the fear
that you might not return, or not for a very long time,
months or years stolen from your life. Roland didn't
tell me all of this. He tried to explain but fear and grief
started to overwhelm him both mentally and physically.

I don't actually remember when he stopped coming
to work completely. I remember he made several unsuc-
cessful attempts to return after taking time off, but he
couldn't escape his intrusive thoughts. Previously
always available to his patients, Roland was now unable
to see through a full appointment. So, he decided to
stay home and focus on fighting your cause. He asked
me to let people know, to explain in clear and simple
terms to the rest of the team what was happening.
Usually such a private person, he asked me to hold a

briefing for all 35 colleagues about your situation. Everyone fell silent at the news, people exchanged glances, the news in all its violence had touched one of our own, one of the team.

Each of Roland's colleagues offered to step up so as to minimise the impact of his absence on the patients. It was a show of solidarity to protect these young people and to reassure each other that we were doing everything we could for Roland, for you, for those fighting oppression.

I have to tell you the deep sadness I felt at the thought of everything the two of you were going through. And I could see that I was not the only one of the team to feel this, especially when you stopped eating, stopped taking medication. That made the start of each day at the hospital very tough, the look on people's faces as they realised that this almost unreal situation was actually happening, and affecting one of our own colleagues, our friend. We began our work exchanging just a few words, not saying very much, but clearly all of us were thinking constantly of you, of the two of you.

And then, pure joy, the incredible sense of relief when we heard the news of your return. The start of a new chapter and the chance finally to have the privilege of meeting you.

Thank you for coming home.
Myriam

A Concert for Bernard

Luce Delucq

It was in February 2023 that Roland came up with the idea of organising a concert for Bernard's liberation. I didn't quite get the idea at first. I began saying, 'Well, of course, to mark his release, we'll have an amazing concert,' but a strange silence followed. The following day, Roland again raised the idea of a concert, as if it was going to happen sooner rather than later. Frankly, I was uncomfortable, as we had no idea when Bernard might ever be released. As carefully as I possibly could, because we were all feeling so upset and fragile at that time, I said, 'Well, sure, my dear Roro . . . but wouldn't Bernard need to have been freed before we could start to plan a freedom concert?' In saying those words, I realised that we could in fact have a concert to work towards his release, not only to celebrate it, and that was what Roland was aiming for. With our intentions clarified, we began to make a plan. Our aim was to shine a media spotlight, in a pacifist manner, on the unjust and inhumane situation that had been imposed on Bernard.

It didn't take long to assemble the team of artists we needed for this solidarity concert. In the space of just a few hours, six of my closest friends, who had been following news of Bernard's hostage situation for months, blocked off the date of 31 March in their diaries: singer and harpist Eva Genniaux, singer Luna Garcia Odin, oboist Ariane Bacquet, cellist Sophie Chauvenet, guitarist Benoît Convert and actor Geoffrey Perrin. Once I knew I could count on their participation, their friendship and their talent, I was sure that this would be both a beautiful and a worthy event. That no matter what, this concert would mark an important moment for those of us who had been reduced to silence and haunted by a heavy sense of powerlessness for the previous six months.

For maximum impact, the concert would be scheduled for the day after the vigil in front of the Iranian embassy in Dublin. We spent time creating a programme that comprised poetry and music, drawing our inspiration from the emails we had been exchanging with Bernard via the crisis team in the Quai d'Orsay: 'What I miss most is music, which can conjure up love, tenderness, nature, the sound of the sea, a sense of joy, a caress, the sound of silence, a woman's voice, a sense of peace . . .' wrote Bernard. So we selected some traditional airs from Ireland and Catalunya, some Fauré, an extract from Olivier Messiaen's 'Quartet for the End of Time', pieces by Britten, Bartok, Rameau, Vivaldi, Poulenc and Chopin, as well as some original compositions, and the poetry of W.B. Yeats.

Some other friends took charge of media relations and the practicalities of the event. We were given a wonderful reception at the magnificent chapel beside the Centre Culturel Irlandais. As musicians, we took the decision to play for Bernard as if he were there in person, and for his loved ones who were suffering so much, in the hope that the sound of our instruments and our voices would give them back some strength, some tenderness and hope, to help to see them through until the moment of his still-hypothetical release.

At the end of the concert, Roland confided to me that he had felt him close by, as if the part of Bernard that was still free was present with us that evening. We closed the concert with the song 'September' by the French singer Barbara, one of Roland's favourite artists: 'May flowers have never looked so beautiful . . . the vines this year will bear the sweetest grapes . . . when you come back to me, with the swallows . . . because you will come back, my love . . . I'll see you tomorrow . . .'

And in May, Bernard returned.

I will never forget this moment in my life, nor any of the people near or far who helped to make it possible. From the bottom of my heart, I thank them as well as all those who find the courage to struggle to defend human dignity in the midst of our chaotic world.

Extracts of the concert are available at: https://vimeo.com/951857363

The Case of Johan Floderus

Bernard Phelan

Johan is an EU employee who was taken prisoner in Tehran, where he had been on holiday visiting friends at the Swedish embassy. He was picked up on his way to the airport on 17 April 2022. His imprisonment became public knowledge only after 500 days. Prior to that, his parents were following instructions from the Swedish Ministry of Foreign Affairs to keep everything under wraps, an exact parallel to what the French authorities implored Roland and Caroline to do regarding my imprisonment. Johan had moved to Brussels in 2015 for an intern position at Sweden's permanent representation at the EU. After a further master's degree in development economics at SOAS, London, he returned to the EU, working as a programme manager at the EU delegation in Afghanistan, based in Brussels.

I met Johan's partner Johnathan for lunch in Paris on 20 November 2023 and he told me his story. Since he and Johan were not married, it had initially been difficult to play an active role in fighting for Johan's release. Johan's parents were, understandably, very afraid of doing anything that might put their son's life in jeopardy, such as 'outing' him. I tried to reassure Johnathan by saying that no physical harm would come to his partner in Iran. The regime has every interest in keeping hostages in good health. However, the mental torture is something else, as I experienced. I also told him that he and the family had to get Johan's story into the media and to start working on persuading the Swedish authorities to do more than just asking everyone to keep quiet. I told Johnathan that I was willing to travel to Sweden to meet Johan's parents in order to reassure them.

A few weeks later, on 2 December, Roland and I went to Brussels to meet Johan's father, Matts, who had travelled from Gothenburg.

We tried to reassure Matts, while also insisting that keeping such a low profile was not going to accelerate his son's release. I told him that he really needed to move to a different level of action. I explained how, for example, the vigil outside the Iranian embassy in Dublin had helped to get my case into not just European headlines but Iranian opposition channels. Matts had an interview with *The Guardian* following our visit, and this was published on 8 December. In the interview, he conceded that 'silent diplomacy was not working', that things were 'better since [Johan's] name became public'.

Things started to move. Johnathan asked me to take part in a press conference in Brussels where Olivier Vandecasteele, a Belgian hostage who was released shortly after me in May 2023, would also speak. A few days ahead of the event, Johnathan organised a video call with all the participants. It was explained that the audience could ask questions via a web tool that allowed the moderators to filter where necessary. We were asked if there were any taboo subjects; for me there were none. This was too important to start saying there were certain things I did not want to talk about.

The event took place on the evening of 1 February 2024 in a packed hall at the Palais des Beaux Arts. Before I went on stage, I gave interviews to some Swedish and Belgian media. A wide range of people were in attendance. I imagine there were a few people from the Iranian embassy present.

Olivier had spent a short time in the same cell as Johan in Evin prison in Tehran, so he was able to describe the conditions of their detention to the audience. He told us how they shared their love of literature and compared notes on their humanitarian work for Iran. There were lots of questions for both of us. I spoke about how Caroline and Roland made sure my case was a priority for both the Irish and French foreign ministries and that, as Roland had said on a number of occasions, the 'fear needs to change sides'. We must not be afraid of the Iranians. They must be afraid of what we tell the world about how they treat their hostages, telling lies, respecting no international convention, ignoring basic human rights. The RTÉ television clip of the vigil at the Iranian embassy in Dublin was shown with the very moving part where my father crosses the road to put a letter in the embassy letter box and turns to speak to the crowd. It got a big round of applause. I was so proud of Caroline and my father.

I asked an open question: was the EU still working with the Iranian regime while one of their diplomats was in prison?

I returned on the last train of the day to Paris exhausted, but happy to have helped get Johan's case more to the forefront in Europe. Johnathan told me the feedback was excellent and that the team was spurred on to do more.

On 14 March, I saw on X (formerly Twitter) that Johan's friends and Olivier had demonstrated in front of the Iranian embassy in Brussels. At last! On 7 February, Johnathan asked me if I would be willing to come to Stockholm for a similar event in March. Olivier would be present, as well as Martin Schibbye, a journalist who had been held in an Ethiopian prison for 438 days in 2011. This time there were to be no questions from the audience. Instead, a well-known media personality, Karin Hübinette, was to interview the three of us. I had a one-to-one video call with her to get acquainted.

The event was held at the Kulturhuset in the very centre of the city. Again it was a packed event. I met Johan's mother, Kerstin Floderus and his sister Tove Floderus, a doctor. Johan's father told me that he still had no 'plan B'. I was not surprised. There were familiar faces from Brussels too. Olivier and I did some interviews with Swedish radio beforehand.

Johan had sent a text in English, via the Swedish embassy in Tehran, to be read out at the event.

After his sisters Ingrid and Tove, and Johan's letter was read out, Olivier, Martin and I came on stage. Karin was excellent in the way she got the three of us to talk about our experiences. One thing that stuck in my mind that she asked us was about the word 'hope' in Johan's letter. All three of us said that in prison, hope was too painful to contemplate. Olivier was able to share his time with Johan, which was very moving.

All three of us insisted that Johan's case must be a priority for the Swedish government. I explained that the letter from the Irish president, Michael D. Higgins, to my father had been translated into Persian and given to me in prison by Justin Ryan, the Irish chargé d'affaires. I asked if the King of Sweden, Carl XVI Gustaf, could write to Johan's parents in a similar manner. It would show the Iranian regime the level of importance that Johan's case had in the country.

I was washed out when I left the stage with the others. As I made my way to the bar, different people came up to me to shake my hand. One man introduced himself as a Chilean whose father had been imprisoned under the Pinochet regime. He introduced me to his wife, who, I learned later, was an Iranian lawyer in Sweden. Then another lawyer introduced himself. He said my suggestion about the king was excellent. I replied that even a letter from the Swedish prime minister, which would be seen by the Iranian authorities, would help Johan's case.

I left early, as I had to give an interview the next morning, with Johan's sisters, Ingrid and Tove, on Swedish breakfast television, and the taxi was at 5.45 a.m. The alarm went off at 4.15 a.m. I had slept very badly but the sun was up, which cheered me a lot.

We met the sisters outside the studios of Swedish TV station TV4. Tove and Ingrid were to be interviewed first by the two hosts. When we walked into the studio, my heart jumped and my hands began to sweat. On one wall was a huge screen displaying the Iranian flag. It was right beside my seat. There was another screen with a picture of Johan with the flag as the background, beside where his sisters would sit. Thankfully, the background was altered and I felt a lot more comfortable.

The interview seemed to go down well, but the memories of my time in Mashhad would come back at the strangest of times. One morning, I went to visit the photographic museum, Fotografiska. There was a video of planes in the sky. I had a flashback to standing in the prison courtyard and seeing the planes taking off from Mashhad airport. I began to panic.

I flew back to Paris on Easter Monday evening.

Johan Floderus was released on 15 June 2024, in exchange for the Iranian prison guard Hamid Nouri, jailed in Stockholm for crimes against humanity in 2019.

A Selection from my Prison Reading List

A Small Death in Lisbon Robert Wilson

Don Quixote Miguel de Cervantes

Letter to a Hostage and *Le Petit Prince* Antoine de Saint-Exupéry.

Regeneration Pat Barker

Silk Alessandro Baricco

The Anomaly Hervé Le Tellier

The Baron in the Trees Italo Calvino

The Chalk Man C. J. Tudor

The Counterfeiters André Gide

The Phone Booth at the Edge of the World Laura Imai Messina

The Thursday Murder Club and *The Man Who Died Twice* Richard Osman

The Truth About the Harry Quebert Affair and *The Baltimore Boys* Joël Dicker

The Twelve Tasks of Astérix Albert Uderzo & René Goscinny

11.22.63 Stephen King

Why We Sleep Matthew Walker

Some Messages Sent During my Incarceration

To Caroline 22/12/2022

Dear Caroline,

Christmas is in a few days and apparently, I am staying in prison. I really appreciate you spending Christmas with Dad in Dublin (I sent you a message for him yesterday).

I am completely desperate for my future here. I am exhausted in my daily battle to be able to call my family, to send letters, to get books, to get my medicine, to find something to eat properly, to figure out how to stay warm. I don't know what to say to you anymore, but I hug you very, very hard

Bernard

P.S. As your appointment is today at the Department of Foreign Affairs in Dublin, I know you can't say much but at least you can tell me if there is anything new or not.

To Roland and Caroline 26/12/2022

I hope you are both well. Thank you for your messages this weekend. I'll get back to you later today.

Here, it is very cold but dry. On the medication side, in the Paris delivery, the LAROXYL and the vitamin D were missing, to be checked with the pharmacy there but not urgent. A nice doctor here gave me an injection for vitamin D, and he will try to get me the equivalent of LAROXYL (it's for sleeping). On the health side, I have the impression that the capsulitis in my left shoulder is advancing into my arm. I have a lot of back and neck pain. I have difficulty turning my head to the left. The worst is my knees, I had an appointment with a rheumatologist in mid-October: the pain is getting worse and worse. It wakes me up at night. I take paracetamol. I continue to have pain in my chest and occasionally like a needle in my back at the same time. Otherwise, we all have problems with our feet here as it's super dry and impossible to get creams, we all have cracks on our feet. I also felt that my eyesight was deteriorating, which is strange following the operation at the beginning of the year. Maybe because I haven't had any treatment for a while.

Hugs to you both,
Bernard

To Caroline 27/12/2022

Dear Caroline,

Thank you for the message. Yes, I can imagine Dad at Christmas and what's more, he watches a lot of television and reads the newspapers every day, that's all he's going to talk about. The sooner this ends, the better. This is exhausting for all of you.

  For Eoghan Corry, I received a message a few weeks ago via the lawyer. She needs to send me a hard copy.

Love,
Bernard

To Caroline and Roland 31/01/2023

Hi,

Do not worry about me. I am taking my medicine, and I am eating. But yesterday, the phone was cut for a very long time, you know the problem. Their 'white torture' works. I break down or I broke down I don't know, and I cried a lot last night.

Bernard

To Roland 9/03/2023

My dear Roland,

Yesterday afternoon, I received messages from people I haven't seen in a long time. I called Justin and before reading my messages to me, he informed me that the Irish government no longer intends to open an embassy in Iran with my current situation.

I imagine you are aware of the press conference in Dublin yesterday and who was there. Location is hyper symbolic because it is the 'hotel' of the Irish National Assembly. We passed by it often.

Hoping who doesn't stay long to find you [*sic*], you have to bring extra, ok? Good triple thickness.

Lots of hugs,
Bernard

To Caroline and Roland 28/03/2024

Hello both of you,

This Tuesday morning, I met the authorities' doctor again, without his colleague. We spoke about this yesterday with M. ROCHE. I'll spare you the details, but he took my blood pressure with a professional instrument (18.6 after my morning measurement), and he examined me again.

I gave him a copy of Dr. CAMPA's latest report and my prescription (both in French and Persian thanks to the embassy). The block director showed him the sheets of my daily blood pressure measurement. I don't really have the impression that he looked. Then DR HANEI joined us. They know each other very well. We talked about all my problems, including the chair incident.

I also informed him that a new treatment for blood pressure is on its way from France. Fingers crossed that this visit will unblock things, as Mr ROCHE thought last night.

That's all, love to you both.

Bernard

UACHTARÁN NA hÉIREANN
PRESIDENT OF IRELAND

Mr. Vincent Phelan
53 Stillorgan Park
Dublin

4th April 2023

Dear Vincent

Thank you for the deeply heartfelt letter, which you sent me earlier this year regarding the extremely distressing situation which your son Bernard continues to face in Iran.

I know that at my request, my Deputy Secretary-General, George Burke, was in touch with you and with your daughter Caroline in January with regard to Bernard's case.

Your letter has remained in my mind; I can readily understand the pain and suffering that you are going through at this difficult time.

I wanted to write to you personally, as I was particularly struck by the dignity with which you, your family and Bernard's supporters have carried out your vigil over the last week. I am anxious to do whatever I can to help in securing Bernard's release.

I have asked the Department of Foreign Affairs, and have had direct conversations with the Tánaiste and Minister for Foreign Affairs, Micheál Martin, asking them to keep me directly updated on any developments in Bernard's case, and I have reiterated that I am available to assist in any additional way which may be deemed helpful in securing Bernard's release.

I know that these are very anxious and most difficult times for you and your family. Be assured that you are in the thoughts and prayers of Sabina and I, and it is our earnest hope that your son, Bernard, will be returned to you safely as soon as possible.

Please don't hesitate to contact me again should you wish to get in touch.

With my very best wishes

Yours sincerely

Michael D. Higgins
Uachtarán na hÉireann
President of Ireland

A Patch of Blue – Greg O'Corry-Crowe

I heard the news the other day
They'd come and taken him away
He took a picture in the rain
They put his face in the frame

A girl had dared to wake Gen Z
Had paid her life for liberty
Protest marches, cops and spooks
They're arresting kids down the souk

Talk about, wrong time, wrong place, buddy!
Solitary, hunger strike
His father woke up in the night
Sister, husband got the call,
They stood alone to face the wall
Southern star to northern lights
They signed on overnight
Light a candle, pass it on
Tell the world what's going on

Jesus, Bernard stay alive!
Caroline, you're on in five
RTE, Tipp FM
Tomorrow, do it all again

Diplomats, Michael D.
Negotiations over tea
Vigils, protests, N.G.O.s
Will we get him out before the snows?

I'll tell you one thing; you don't want to mess with the
mommas!
Inside, the walls were closing in
Time slipped by, the light grew dim
Don't you dare, you must pull through
Behind the clouds, a patch of blue

Outside, a cry to set him free
Up the ante, make a deal
Then after months of endless talk
We won't forget you let him walk

The Irish never played the Game
Tread the earth, treat all the same

Why can't we just agree,
That you do you,
. . . and I'll do me.

Acknowledgements

Thanks to Micheál Martin, Simon Coveney, Leo Varadkar and the many elected representatives, European, national and local, who put their shoulder to the wheel and took time out of their busy lives to advocate on my behalf. I would also, in particular like to thank both Sonya McGuinness, the Irish ambassador, at the time, to Iran and her colleague Justin Ryan for being so patient and always ready to listen. Amnesty International Ireland, whose Dún Laoghaire branch started protesting outside the Iranian embassy from January 2023, thank you.

I would also like to warmly thank Nicolas Roche and Ahmeneh Ershadi at the French embassy in Tehran for their dedication and valuable help.

A further thanks to the following people for their help with this book:

Greg Corry-Crow, David Craig, Emilie Craig, Marie-Martine Dorain, Myriam Frégonèse, Lisa Gilmour, Patricia Glennie, Declan Heeney, Simon Hess, Niamh Kinsella, Lara Marlowe, Brian McColgan, Gerry McColgan, Dara McMahon, Deirdre Nolan, Kathy Phelan, Olivia Renshaw, Susan Spindler and Alison Walsh.